D1316411

Your Complete Guide to Jello Shots! ®

By

Aaron Wright

LAYOUT AND DESIGN BY VINA WEB CO.
WWW.VINAWEBCO.COM

AVERAGE JOE PUBLISHING

WWW.AVERAGEJOEPUBLISHING.COM

YOUR COMPLETE GUIDE TO JELLO SHOTS! ™

ISBN-13 978-0-9792553-1-1
ISBN-10 0-979-2553-1-7

Average Joe Publishing
P.O. Box 2982 Clackamas Or. 97015

www.averagejoepublishing.com

www.yourcompleteguidetojelloshots.com

Disclaimer

Your Complete guide to Jello Shots™ is intended for audiences of legal drinking age who wish to explore and experience the novelty of gelatin cocktails.

The author, publisher, their agents, officers, employees, wholesalers, distributors, retailers and /or any other persons associated with this book do not advocate the abuse or misuse of alcoholic beverages & urge anyone using the recipes contained herein to do so with moderation and extreme caution.

The material in this book is for entertainment purposes. Please consult with your local, state, and federal laws/regulations prior to executing any of the recipes in this book. By reviewing the material in this book, you agree to hold harmless the author, publisher, their agents, officers, employees, wholesalers, distributors, and retailers from any and all liability or claim that may arise due to the direct or indirect use of the material within or any variation there-of.

Never Drink and Drive!

Table of contents

Introduction

Welcome to the wonderful world of Jello Shots! Often times reffered to as Jello shooters. As many college campuses, bars, nightclubs, private parties and social gatherings across the world have discovered, Jello shots are great for any kind of adult party or get-together. They add a flaver and smoothness to your favorite spirit or cocktail like nothing else you've ever experienced!

Jello was first patented in 1845 by a fellow named Peter Cooper. Cooper later sold the patent to a visionary named Pearl B Waite who created the first fruit flavored version of Jello. The first JELLO SHOT wasn't introduced until the early 1900's when a college drop-out by the name of Orator Francis Woodward got his hands on the patent for a small fortune of $450. Losing faith in his idea, he almost sold the patent for $39, but started seeing a dramatic increase in sales and decided to keep it. By the early 1920's Jello became a household name.

This book will guide you through every step of the way in making your own Jello shots. We have compiled a list of over 300 great Jello shot recipes! But truly the list is only limited by your imagination!

What is a Jello shot?

A Jello shot is simply a Jello cocktail, an alcoholic beverage made using a combination of your favorite alcohol, hot and cold water, and your favorite Gelatin. Jello shots are usually made in 2-3 oz containers to resemble a "shot" of alcohol you would be served in a bar or restaurant.

Basic Recipe

The basic recipe for Jello shots is to substitute ¼ of the total water the Jello/gelatin recipe on the box calls for with the alcohol(s) of your choice. And continue to follow the Jello/Gelatin box instructions. Choosing a 2 oz container (recommended) you will have an alcohol content of .5 oz per shot. The average alcohol content of a shot of liquor served in a bar or restaurant is 1.25 - 1.75 oz.

You may increase the amount of liquor in your Jello shots by increasing the liquor and decreasing the same amount of water the recipe calls for. Simply adding liquor and not reducing an equal amount of water may make your Jello shot too runny and may not set properly.

Be careful!! Jello shots are very deceiving! And addictive! Just because you can't taste that much alcohol, doesn't mean it's not in there!

As with any alcoholic beverage, Drink responsibly and inform your guests of the alcohol content in your Jello shots. Moderation is essential with Jello shots!

Jello=Gelatin

For the purposes of this book Jello and Gelatin mean the same thing. You may use any brand of Gelatin/Jello you prefer.

of Jello shots per batch

At the time of this publication, most gelatin is sold in both a six ounce box and a three ounce box. The six ounce box produces 16-20 2oz Jello shots using the basic recipe in this book and the three ounce box produces 8-10 2oz Jello shots using the basic recipe in this book.

When throwing a party, it's difficult to plan for how many Jello shots you'll need. I generally prepare 4-6 Jello shots for each guest. They are an amazing icebreaker!

To make larger quantities, check with your local restaurant supplier for larger *bulk* Packages of gelatin. Keep in mind the basic recipe in this book and you will be in good shape!

Jello Shot Containers

Half the fun of Jello Shots is watching your guests get them out of small containers! Here are a few suggestions that have been very popular in the past.

-2 oz silo containers with lids found at any restaurant supply store. Getting the Jello out is a little work. Use a toothpick and separate the jello from the sides in a circular motion then suck it out! Some people dip the bottom of the cup in hot water loosening the jello from the inside.

-Some people prefer to use the paper ketchup containers Like the ones at Mcdonalds because you can rip the container and suck the jello out! These too are found at your local grocery store or restaurant supply store

-For small parties, I will use fruit halves. Take your desired fruit, lemons, limes, oranges (anything with a tough skin) Cut it in half, scrape out the fruit (you can either throw the fruit away or add some of it to your Jelloshots for added txture) and fill them with your Jello mixture (put the filled halves in muffin pans to set in the fridge with no spills). When they set up, cut the halves in half again making quarter wedges. They look cool and Taste great!

-Jello Injectors! (Syringes!) A great party hit is to fill Jello Injectors with your Jello shots, Then just squeeze the plunger! The best part is that these ones are re-usable! 60 cc Medical syringes work well for this, they are just over 2 oz, but they can be a little expensive. Jello Injectors can be purchased very reasonably online at www.shotskis.com you'll also find a great variety of other useful party supplies!

-Ice cube trays. The tough part about using ice cube trays is getting the finished Jello shots out of the trays. Try spraying the trays with cooking spray beforehand. Or just dip the bottom of the ice cube tray in hot water when you are ready to take them out. The hot water will melt the Jello on the bottom and sides making them slide out. Be careful not to leave them in the water too long! 5-10 seconds is usually enough depending on how hot your water is.

-Shot Glasses! Shot Glasses, although obvious, are an often overlooked option. Use a Toothpick around the edge to get them out or dip the shot glass in hot water just before serving.

-Jello/Candy molds. Depending on what you are doing with your Jello shots, traditional Jello molds or candy molds might be an option for you. Most cake decorating supply stores will have a variety of molds for almost any theme or idea for you to choose from.

Measurement table

Below is a measurement conversion table for your convienence

Liquid Measure Conversion
Liquid Measure Conversion

gal	qt	pt	cup	fl oz	tbsp	tsp
				1/2 fl oz =	1 tbsp =	3 tsp
			1/8 cup	1 fl oz	2 tbsp	6 tbs
			1/4 cup	2 fl oz	4 tbsp	12 tbs
			1/2 cup	4 fl oz	8 tbsp	24 tbs
	1/4 qt	1/2 pt	1 cup	8 fl oz		
	1/2 gal	1 pt	2 cups	16 fl oz		
1/4 gal	1 qt	2 pt	4 cups	32 fl oz		
1/2 gal	2 qt	4 pt	8 cups	64 fl oz		
1 gal	4 qt	8 pt	16 cups	128 fl oz		

Helpful Tips

1.   Serving Jello Shots in a large container (bowl) is not recommended. The alcohol settles to the bottom and does not gellify, making a great big mess!
2.   Add a little whipped cream to the top of your Jello Shots when serving. Yum!
3.   Add cut up fruit to your Jello Shots for added flavor and texture.
4.   Watching Carbs? Try using Sugar free Jello.
5.   For a decorative touch, add a gummy bear to your shot when chilling.
6.   For extra firmness, add a package of unflavored geletin.
7.   Add ½ cup club soda in place of water for a champagne fizz.
8.   Substitute apple juice for the hot water (heat to just before boiling) to increase sweetness
9.   Alcohol evaporates at 170° so let your boiled water cool a little before adding

10.   alcohol or else you will evaporate your alcohol.

Layering

Layering is a very cool way to present your Jello shots (if your Jello shot containers are transparent). To layer your Jello shot, simply make a few different colors of Jello shot mix and add one color on top of another after it has set. Red, white and blue shots are great for 4th of July parties, political events etc. Making Jello shots layered in your favorite team colors makes for a great sporting event. The trick to layering is to make your different Jello mixtures about ten minutes apart. Wait just long enough for a skin to form on the Jello surface before adding the second color. Allow the second color and additional colors to cool a little, and form a skin before layering them. Adding hot Jello to cool Jello will melt the underlying Jello and mix the colors. This may take a few tries, but you'll get the hang of it.

Jello Shot Recipes

The Jello shot recipes in this book are organized by the alcohol in them. A Jello shot with more than one alcohol will be listed under each alcohol contained for easy reference.

The recipes in this book are assuming you are using the three ounce package of gelatin (unless noted), if you prefer the six ounce package, simply double the other ingredients. Good luck! Drink responsibly! And have fun!!

Amaretto

Amaretto

Midnight Affair

3 oz pkg Black Cherry Jello
1 cup boiling water
½ cup cold water
½ cup AMARETTO

Mix Gelatin with hot water until dissolved (approx 2 minutes). Add cold water, stir. Let sit until steam dissipates (no more than three minutes). Add Alcohol, Stir thoroughly (1-2 minutes). Pour mixture into your chosen Jello shot containers. Refrigerate for 4 hours or until firm. Makes 8-10 2oz Jello shots.

Daydream

3 oz pkg Pineapple Jello
1 cup boiling water
½ cup cold water
½ cup AMARETTO

Mix Gelatin with hot water until dissolved (approx 2 minutes). Add cold water, stir. Let sit until steam dissipates (no more than three minutes). Add Alcohol, Stir thoroughly (1-2 minutes). Pour mixture into your chosen Jello shot containers. Refrigerate for 4 hours or until firm. Makes 8-10 2oz Jello shots.

Broken Down Golf Cart

3 oz pkg Cranberry Jello
1 cup boiling water
½ cup cold water
¼ cup VODKA
¼ cup AMARETTO

Mix Gelatin with hot water until dissolved (approx 2 minutes). Add cold water, stir. Let sit until steam dissipates (no more than three minutes). Add Alcohol, Stir thoroughly (1-2 minutes). Pour mixture into your chosen Jello shot containers. Refrigerate for 4 hours or until firm. Makes 8-10 2oz Jello shots.

Amaretto

Panty Dropper

6 oz pkg Cherry Jello (or two 3 oz packages)
1 cup boiling water
½ cup cold water
½ cup cola
½ cup VODKA
½ cup SOUTHERN COMFORT
1/3 cup DARK RUM
1/3 cup AMARETTO
1/3 cup TEQUILLA

Mix Gelatin with hot water until dissolved (approx 2 minutes). Add cold water and cola, stir. Let sit until steam dissipates (no more than three minutes). Add Alcohol, Stir thoroughly (1-2 minutes). Pour mixture into your chosen Jello shot containers. Refrigerate for 4 hours or until firm. Makes 16-20 2oz Jello shots.

Sun Kiss

3 oz pkg Orange Jello
1 cup boiling water
½ cup cold water
½ cup AMARETTO

Mix Gelatin with hot water until dissolved (approx 2 minutes). Add cold water, stir. Let sit until steam dissipates (no more than three minutes). Add Alcohol, Stir thoroughly (1-2 minutes). Pour mixture into your chosen Jello shot containers. Refrigerate for 4 hours or until firm. Makes 8-10 2oz Jello shots.

Puppy Love

3 oz pkg Apricot Jello
1 cup boiling water
½ cup cold water
½ cup AMARETTO

Mix Gelatin with hot water until dissolved (approx 2 minutes). Add cold water, stir. Let sit until steam dissipates (no more than three minutes). Add Alcohol, Stir thoroughly (1-2 minutes). Pour mixture into your chosen Jello shot containers. Refrigerate for 4 hours or until firm. Makes 8-10 2oz Jello shots.

Amaretto

Caribbean Romance

3oz pkg Orange Jello
1 cup boiling water
¼ cup cold water
¼ cup Grenedine
¼ cup AMARETTO
¼ cup PINEAPPLE RUM

Mix Gelatin with hot water until dissolved (approx 2 minutes). Add cold water, stir. Let sit until steam dissipates (no more than three minutes). Add Grenedine and Alcohol, Stir thoroughly (1-2 minutes). Pour mixture into your chosen Jello shot containers. Refrigerate for 4 hours or until firm. Makes 8-10 2oz Jello shots.

Komaniwanalaya

3 oz pkg Pineapple Jello
3 oz pkg Cranberry Jello
2 cups boiling water
1 cup cold water
½ cup AMARETTO
½ cup 151 RUM

Mix Gelatin with hot water until dissolved (approx 2 minutes). Add cold water, stir. Let sit until steam dissipates (no more than three minutes). Add Alcohol, Stir thoroughly (1-2 minutes). Pour mixture into your chosen Jello shot containers. Refrigerate for 4 hours or until firm. Makes 16-20 2oz Jello shots.

Peckerhead

3 oz pkg Pineapple Jello
1 cup boiling water
½ cup cold water
¼ cup SOUTHERN COMFORT
¼ cup AMARETTO

Mix Gelatin with hot water until dissolved (approx 2 minutes). Add cold water, stir. Let sit until steam dissipates (no more than three minutes). Add Alcohol, Stir thoroughly (1-2 minutes). Pour mixture into your chosen Jello shot containers. Refrigerate for 4 hours or until firm. Makes 8-10 2oz Jello shots.

Amaretto

Rocky Mountain

3oz pkg Lime Jello
1 cup boiling water
¼ cup cold water
¼ cup AMARETTO
¼ cup SOUTHERN COMFORT

Mix Gelatin with hot water until dissolved (approx 2 minutes). Add cold water, stir. Let sit until steam dissipates (no more than three minutes). Add Alcohol, Stir thoroughly (1-2 minutes). Pour mixture into your chosen Jello shot containers. Refrigerate for 4 hours or until firm. Makes 8-10 2oz Jello shots.

Italian Surfer

3 oz pkg Pineapple Jello
1 cup boiling water
¼ cup cold water
¼ cup AMARETTO
¼ cup BRANDY

Mix Gelatin with hot water until dissolved (approx 2 minutes). Add cold water, stir. Let sit until steam dissipates (no more than three minutes). Add Alcohol, Stir thoroughly (1-2 minutes). Pour mixture into your chosen Jello shot containers. Refrigerate for 4 hours or until firm. Makes 8-10 2oz Jello shots.

Alabama Slammer

3 oz pkg lemon Jello
¾ cup boiling water
½ cup cold water
¼ cup AMARETTO
¼ cup SOUTHERN COMFORT
¼ cup SLOE GIN

Mix Gelatin with hot water until dissolved (approx 2 minutes). Add cold water, stir. Let sit until steam dissipates (no more than three minutes). Add Alcohol, Stir thoroughly (1-2 minutes). Pour mixture into your chosen Jello shot containers. Refrigerate for 4 hours or until firm. Makes 8-10 2oz Jello shots.

Amaretto

Jager-Master

3 oz pkg Orange Jello
1 cup boiling water
½ cup cold water
splash of Grenedine
¼ cup AMARETTO
¼ cup JAGERMEISTER

Mix Gelatin with hot water until dissolved (approx 2 minutes). Add cold water, stir. Let sit until steam dissipates (no more than three minutes). Add Alcohol, Stir thoroughly (1-2 minutes). Pour mixture into your chosen Jello shot containers. Refrigerate for 4 hours or until firm. Makes 8-10 2oz Jello shots.

Lethal Injection

3 oz pkg Orange Jello
3 oz pkg Pineapple Jello
2 cups boiling water
1 cup cold water
¼ cup AMARETTO
¼ cup DARK RUM
¼ cup SPICED RUM
¼ cup COCONUT RUM

Mix Gelatin with hot water until dissolved (approx 2 minutes). Add cold water, stir. Let sit until steam dissipates (no more than three minutes). Add Alcohol, Stir thoroughly (1-2 minutes). Pour mixture into your chosen Jello shot containers. Refrigerate for 4 hours or until firm. Makes 16-20 2oz Jello shots.

Brandy

Brandy

Beauty Mark

3 oz pkg Cherry Jello
1 cup boiling water
½ cup cold water
½ cup BRANDY

Mix Gelatin with hot water until dissolved (approx 2 minutes). Add cold water, stir. Let sit until steam dissipates (no more than three minutes). Add Alcohol, Stir thoroughly (1-2 minutes). Pour mixture into your chosen Jello shot containers. Refrigerate for 4 hours or until firm. Makes 8-10 2oz Jello shots.

Ankle Breaker

3 oz pkg Lime Jello
1 cup boiling water
½ cup cold water
¼ cup 151 RUM
¼ cup CHERY BRANDY

Mix Gelatin with hot water until dissolved (approx 2 minutes). Add cold water, stir. Let sit until steam dissipates (no more than three minutes). Add Alcohol, Stir thoroughly (1-2 minutes). Pour mixture into your chosen Jello shot containers. Refrigerate for 4 hours or until firm. Makes 8-10 2oz Jello shots.

Before and After

3 oz pkg Orange Jello
1 cup boiling water
½ cup cold water
½ cup BRANDY

Mix Gelatin with hot water until dissolved (approx 2 minutes). Add cold water, stir. Let sit until steam dissipates (no more than three minutes). Add Alcohol, Stir thoroughly (1-2 minutes). Pour mixture into your chosen Jello shot containers. Refrigerate for 4 hours or until firm. Makes 8-10 2oz Jello shots.

Brandy

Black Prince

3 oz pkg Lime Jello
1 cup boiling water
½ cup cold water
¼ cup BRANDY
¼ cup CHAMPAGNE

Mix Gelatin with hot water until dissolved (approx 2 minutes). Add cold water, stir. Let sit until steam dissipates (no more than three minutes). Add Alcohol, Stir thoroughly (1-2 minutes). Pour mixture into your chosen Jello shot containers. Refrigerate for 4 hours or until firm. Makes 8-10 2oz Jello shots.

Pancho Villa

3 oz pkg Pineapple Jello
¾ cup boiling water
¼ cup cold water
¼ cup RUM
¼ cup GIN
¼ cup APRICOT BRANDY
¼ cup CHERRY BRANDY

Mix Gelatin with hot water until dissolved (approx 2 minutes). Add cold water, stir. Let sit until steam dissipates (no more than three minutes). Add Alcohol, Stir thoroughly (1-2 minutes). Pour mixture into your chosen Jello shot containers. Refrigerate for 4 hours or until firm. Makes 8-10 2oz Jello shots.

Major Tom

3 oz pkg Orange Jello
¾ cup boiling water
¼ cup cold water
1/3 cup CHERRY VODKA
1/3 cup TRIPLE SEC
1/3 cup CHERRY BRANDY

Mix Gelatin with hot water until dissolved (approx 2 minutes). Add cold water, stir. Let sit until steam dissipates (no more than three minutes). Add Alcohol, Stir thoroughly (1-2 minutes). Pour mixture into your chosen Jello shot containers. Refrigerate for 4 hours or until firm. Makes 8-10 2oz Jello shots.

Brandy

Soft Velvet Kiss

3 oz pkg Grape Jello
1 cup boiling water
½ cup cold water
½ cup BLACKBERRY BRANDY

Mix Gelatin with hot water until dissolved (approx 2 minutes). Add cold water, stir. Let sit until steam dissipates (no more than three minutes). Add Alcohol, Stir thoroughly (1-2 minutes). Pour mixture into your chosen Jello shot containers. Refrigerate for 4 hours or until firm. Makes 8-10 2oz Jello shots.

Chi-Chi

3 oz pkg Pineapple Jello
1 cup boiling water
½ cup cold water
¼ cup BLACKBERRY BRANDY
¼ cup RUM

Mix Gelatin with hot water until dissolved (approx 2 minutes). Add cold water, stir. Let sit until steam dissipates (no more than three minutes). Add Alcohol, Stir thoroughly (1-2 minutes). Pour mixture into your chosen Jello shot containers. Refrigerate for 4 hours or until firm. Makes 8-10 2oz Jello shots.

Italian Surfer

3 oz pkg Pineapple Jello
1 cup boiling water
½ cup cold water
¼ cup BRANDY
¼ cup AMARETTO

Mix Gelatin with hot water until dissolved (approx 2 minutes). Add cold water, stir. Let sit until steam dissipates (no more than three minutes). Add Alcohol, Stir thoroughly (1-2 minutes). Pour mixture into your chosen Jello shot containers. Refrigerate for 4 hours or until firm. Makes 8-10 2oz Jello shots.

Brandy

Adam and Eve

3 oz pkg Lemon Jello
¾ cup boiling water
½ cup cold water
¼ cup BRANDY
¼ cup FORBIDDEN FRUIT LICQOUR
¼ cup GIN

Mix Gelatin with hot water until dissolved (approx 2 minutes). Add cold water, stir. Let sit until steam dissipates (no more than three minutes). Add Alcohol, Stir thoroughly (1-2 minutes). Pour mixture into your chosen Jello shot containers. Refrigerate for 4 hours or until firm. Makes 8-10 2oz Jello shots.

After Dinner Shot

3 oz pkg Lime Jello
1 cup boiling water
½ cup cold water
¼ cup APRICOT FLAVORED BRANDY
¼ cup TRIPLE SEC

Mix Gelatin with hot water until dissolved (approx 2 minutes). Add cold water, stir. Let sit until steam dissipates (no more than three minutes). Add Alcohol, Stir thoroughly (1-2 minutes). Pour mixture into your chosen Jello shot containers. Refrigerate for 4 hours or until firm. Makes 8-10 2oz Jello shots.

Pixie Stick

3 oz pkg Lemon Jello
1 cup boiling water
½ cup cold water
¼ cup SOUTHERN COMFORT
¼ cup BLACKBERRY BRANDY

Mix Gelatin with hot water until dissolved (approx 2 minutes). Add cold water, stir. Let sit until steam dissipates (no more than three minutes). Add Alcohol, Stir thoroughly (1-2 minutes). Pour mixture into your chosen Jello shot containers. Refrigerate for 4 hours or until firm. Makes 8-10 2oz Jello shots.

Brandy

Charlie Chaplin

3 oz pkg Lemon Jello
1 cup boiling water
½ cup cold water
¼ cup APRICOT FLAVORED BRANDY
¼ cup SLOE GIN

Mix Gelatin with hot water until dissolved (approx 2 minutes). Add cold water, stir. Let sit until steam dissipates (no more than three minutes). Add Alcohol, Stir thoroughly (1-2 minutes). Pour mixture into your chosen Jello shot containers. Refrigerate for 4 hours or until firm. Makes 8-10 2oz Jello shots.

Boston Sidecar

3 oz pkg Lime Jello
1 cup boiling water
¼ cup cold water
¼ cup BRANDY
¼ cup LIGHT RUM
¼ cup TRIPLE SEC

Mix Gelatin with hot water until dissolved (approx 2 minutes). Add cold water, stir. Let sit until steam dissipates (no more than three minutes). Add Alcohol, Stir thoroughly (1-2 minutes). Pour mixture into your chosen Jello shot containers. Refrigerate for 4 hours or until firm. Makes 8-10 2oz Jello shots.

Grand Marnier

3 oz pkg Orange Jello
1 cup boiling water
½ cup cold water
¼ cup BRANDY
¼ cup ORANGE COGNAC

Mix Gelatin with hot water until dissolved (approx 2 minutes). Add cold water, stir. Let sit until steam dissipates (no more than three minutes). Add Alcohol, Stir thoroughly (1-2 minutes). Pour mixture into your chosen Jello shot containers. Refrigerate for 4 hours or until firm. Makes 8-10 2oz Jello shots.

Brandy

Loud Speaker

3 oz pkg Lemon Jello
¾ cup boiling water
¼ cup cold water
1/3 cup GIN
1/3 cup BRANDY
1/3 cup ORANGE LIQUEUR

Mix Gelatin with hot water until dissolved (approx 2 minutes). Add cold water, stir. Let sit until steam dissipates (no more than three minutes). Add Alcohol, Stir thoroughly (1-2 minutes). Pour mixture into your chosen Jello shot containers. Refrigerate for 4 hours or until firm. Makes 16-20 2oz Jello shots.

Between the Sheets

3 oz pkg Lemon Jello
¾ cup boiling water
½ cup cold water
¼ cup BRANDY
¼ cup TRIPLE SEC
¼ cup LIGHT RUM

Mix Gelatin with hot water until dissolved (approx 2 minutes). Add cold water, stir. Let sit until steam dissipates (no more than three minutes). Add Alcohol, Stir thoroughly (1-2 minutes). Pour mixture into your chosen Jello shot containers. Refrigerate for 4 hours or until firm. Makes 8-10 2oz Jello shots.

Apple Pie

6 oz pkg Lemon Jello (or two 3 oz packages)
1 ½ cup boiling water
1 cup cold water
½ cup LIGHT RUM
½ cup SWEET VERMOUTH
¼ cup APPLE BRANDY
¼ cup Grenadine

Mix Gelatin with hot water until dissolved (approx 2 minutes). Add cold water, stir. Let sit until steam dissipates (no more than three minutes). Add grenadine and Alcohol, Stir thoroughly (1-2 minutes). Pour mixture into your chosen Jello shot containers. Refrigerate for 4 hours or until firm. Makes 16-20 2oz Jello shots.

__Brandy__

Polynesian Cocktail

3 oz Lime Jello
1 cup boiling water
¼ cup cold water
½ cup VODKA
¼ cup BRANDY

Mix Gelatin with hot water until dissolved (approx 2 minutes). Add cold water, stir. Let sit until steam dissipates (no more than three minutes). Add Alcohol, Stir thoroughly (1-2 minutes). Pour mixture into your chosen Jello shot containers. Refrigerate for 4 hours or until firm. Makes 8-10 2oz Jello shots.

Champagne

Champagne

Peach Fizz

3 oz pkg Peach Jello
1 cup boiling water
½ cup cold water
½ cup EXTRA DRY CHAMPAGNE

Mix Gelatin with hot water until dissolved (approx 2 minutes). Add cold water, stir. Let sit until steam dissipates (no more than three minutes). Add Alcohol, Stir thoroughly (1-2 minutes). Pour mixture into your chosen Jello shot containers. Refrigerate for 4 hours or until firm. Makes 8-10 2oz Jello shots.

Strawberry Fizz

3 oz pkg Strawberry Jello
1 cup boiling water
½ cup cold water
½ cup EXTRA DRY CHAMPAGNE

Mix Gelatin with hot water until dissolved (approx 2 minutes). Add cold water, stir. Let sit until steam dissipates (no more than three minutes). Add Alcohol, Stir thoroughly (1-2 minutes). Pour mixture into your chosen Jello shot containers. Refrigerate for 4 hours or until firm. Makes 8-10 2oz Jello shots.

Mimosa

3 oz pkg Orange Jello
1 cup boiling water
½ cup cold water
½ cup EXTRA DRY CHAMPAGNE

Mix Gelatin with hot water until dissolved (approx 2 minutes). Add cold water, stir. Let sit until steam dissipates (no more than three minutes). Add Alcohol, Stir thoroughly (1-2 minutes). Pour mixture into your chosen Jello shot containers. Refrigerate for 4 hours or until firm. Makes 8-10 2oz Jello shots.

Champagne

Black Prince

3 oz pkg Lime Jello
1 cup boiling water
½ cup cold water
¼ cup BRANDY
¼ cup CHAMPAGNE

Mix Gelatin with hot water until dissolved (approx 2 minutes). Add cold water, stir. Let sit until steam dissipates (no more than three minutes). Add Alcohol, Stir thoroughly (1-2 minutes). Pour mixture into your chosen Jello shot containers. Refrigerate for 4 hours or until firm. Makes 8-10 2oz Jello shots.

Everclear

Everclear and Vodka are pretty much interchangeable. Everclear has a bit more of a kick than vodka, if you are an Everclear fan, you can pretty much substitute Everclear for straight Vodka in any of these recipes. Good Luck! And please Drink responsibly!!

GIN

GIN

Green Devil

3 oz pkg Lime Jello
1 cup boiling water
½ cup cold water
¼ cup GIN
¼ cup CRÈME DE MENTHE

Mix Gelatin with hot water until dissolved (approx 2 minutes). Add cold water, stir. Let sit until steam dissipates (no more than three minutes). Add Alcohol, Stir thoroughly (1-2 minutes). Pour mixture into your chosen Jello shot containers. Refrigerate for 4 hours or until firm. Makes 8-10 2oz Jello shots.

Park Avenue

3 oz pkg Pineapple Jello
1 cup boiling water
¼ cup cold water
½ cup GIN
¼ cup SWEET VERMOUTH

Mix Gelatin with hot water until dissolved (approx 2 minutes). Add cold water, stir. Let sit until steam dissipates (no more than three minutes). Add Alcohol, Stir thoroughly (1-2 minutes). Pour mixture into your chosen Jello shot containers. Refrigerate for 4 hours or until firm. Makes 8-10 2oz Jello shots.

English Screwdriver

3 oz pkg Orange Jello
1 cup boiling water
½ cup cold water
½ cup GIN

Mix Gelatin with hot water until dissolved (approx 2 minutes). Add cold water, stir. Let sit until steam dissipates (no more than three minutes). Add Alcohol, Stir thoroughly (1-2 minutes). Pour mixture into your chosen Jello shot containers. Refrigerate for 4 hours or until firm. Makes 8-10 2oz Jello shots.

GIN

Pancho Villa

3 oz pkg Pineapple Jello
¾ cup boiling water
¼ cup cold water
¼ cup RUM
¼ cup GIN
¼ cup APRICOT BRANDY
¼ cup CHERRY BRANDY

Mix Gelatin with hot water until dissolved (approx 2 minutes). Add cold water, stir. Let sit until steam dissipates (no more than three minutes). Add Alcohol, Stir thoroughly (1-2 minutes). Pour mixture into your chosen Jello shot containers. Refrigerate for 4 hours or until firm. Makes 8-10 2oz Jello shots.

Firecracker

3 oz pkg Orange Jello
¾ cup boiling water
¼ cup cold water
1/3 cup SPICED RUM
1/3 cup SLOE GIN
1/3 cup 151 RUM

Mix Gelatin with hot water until dissolved (approx 2 minutes). Add cold water, stir. Let sit until steam dissipates (no more than three minutes). Add Alcohol, Stir thoroughly (1-2 minutes). Pour mixture into your chosen Jello shot containers. Refrigerate for 4 hours or until firm. Makes 8-10 2oz Jello shots.

Hawaiian Sunrise

3 oz pkg Pineapple Jello
1 cup boiling water
½ cup cold water
¼ cup GIN
¼ cup TRIPLE SEC

Mix Gelatin with hot water until dissolved (approx 2 minutes). Add cold water, stir. Let sit until steam dissipates (no more than three minutes). Add Alcohol, Stir thoroughly (1-2 minutes). Pour mixture into your chosen Jello shot containers. Refrigerate for 4 hours or until firm. Makes 8-10 2oz Jello shots!

GIN

Mac Daddy

3 oz pkg Pineapple Jello
1 cup boiling water
½ cup cold water
¼ cup GIN
¼ cup CHERRY LIQUEUR

Mix Gelatin with hot water until dissolved (approx 2 minutes). Add cold water, stir. Let sit until steam dissipates (no more than three minutes). Add Alcohol, Stir thoroughly (1-2 minutes). Pour mixture into your chosen Jello shot containers. Refrigerate for 4 hours or until firm. Makes 8-10 2oz Jello shots.

Killer Koolaide

6 oz pkg Cranberry Jello (or two 3 oz packages)
1 ½ cups boiling water
¾ cup cold water
½ cup VODKA
½ cup GIN
¼ cup RUM
¼ cup CHAMBORG
¼ cup TRIPLE SEC

Mix Gelatin with hot water until dissolved (approx 2 minutes). Add cold water, stir. Let sit until steam dissipates (no more than three minutes). Add Alcohol, Stir thoroughly (1-2 minutes). Pour mixture into your chosen Jello shot containers. Refrigerate for 4 hours or until firm. Makes 16-20 2oz Jello shots.

Sloe Driver

3 oz pkg Orange Jello
1 cup boiling water
½ cup cold water
½ cup SLOE GIN

Mix Gelatin with hot water until dissolved (approx 2 minutes). Add cold water, stir. Let sit until steam dissipates (no more than three minutes). Add Alcohol, Stir thoroughly (1-2 minutes). Pour mixture into your chosen Jello shot containers. Refrigerate for 4 hours or until firm. Makes 8-10 2oz Jello shots.

GIN

Alabama Slammer

3 oz pkg Lemon Jello
¾ cup boiling water
½ cup cold water
¼ cup GIN
¼ cup SOUTHERN COMFORT
¼ cup AMARETTO

Mix Gelatin with hot water until dissolved (approx 2 minutes). Add cold water, stir. Let sit until steam dissipates (no more than three minutes). Add Alcohol, Stir thoroughly (1-2 minutes). Pour mixture into your chosen Jello shot containers. Refrigerate for 4 hours or until firm. Makes 8-10 2oz Jello shots.

Charlie Chaplin

3 oz pkg Lemon Jello
1 cup boiling water
½ cup cold water
¼ cup SLOE GIN
¼ cup APRICOT FLAVORED BRANDY

Mix Gelatin with hot water until dissolved (approx 2 minutes). Add cold water, stir. Let sit until steam dissipates (no more than three minutes). Add Alcohol, Stir thoroughly (1-2 minutes). Pour mixture into your chosen Jello shot containers. Refrigerate for 4 hours or until firm. Makes 8-10 2oz Jello shots.

Adam and Eve

3 oz pkg Lemon Jello
¾ cup boiling water
½ cup cold water
¼ cup BRANDY
¼ cup FORBIDDEN FRUIT LICQOUR
¼ cup GIN

Mix Gelatin with hot water until dissolved (approx 2 minutes). Add cold water, stir. Let sit until steam dissipates (no more than three minutes). Add Alcohol, Stir thoroughly (1-2 minutes). Pour mixture into your chosen Jello shot containers. Refrigerate for 4 hours or until firm. Makes 8-10 2oz Jello shots.

GIN

Gentle Ben

3 oz pkg Orange Jello
¾ cup boiling water
½ cup cold water
¼ cup GIN
¼ cup TEQUILA
¼ cup VODKA

Mix Gelatin with hot water until dissolved (approx 2 minutes). Add cold water, stir. Let sit until steam dissipates (no more than three minutes). Add Alcohol, Stir thoroughly (1-2 minutes). Pour mixture into your chosen Jello shot containers. Refrigerate for 4 hours or until firm. Makes 8-10 2oz Jello shots.

Long Island Iced Tea

6 oz pkg Lemon Jello (or two 3 oz packages)
1 cup boiling water
½ cup cola
½ cup cold water
½ cup GIN
½ cup LIGHT RUM
½ cup VODKA
½ cup TEQUILA

Mix Gelatin with hot water until dissolved (approx 2 minutes). Add cold water and cola, stir. Let sit until steam dissipates (no more than three minutes). Add Alcohol, Stir thoroughly (1-2 minutes). Pour mixture into your chosen Jello shot containers. Refrigerate for 4 hours or until firm. Makes 16-20 2oz Jello shots.

Ninja Turtle

3 oz pkg Orange Jello
1 cup boiling water
½ cup cold water
¼ cup GIN
¼ cup BLUE CURACOA

Mix Gelatin with hot water until dissolved (approx 2 minutes). Add cold water, stir. Let sit until steam dissipates (no more than three minutes). Add Alcohol, Stir thoroughly (1-2 minutes). Pour mixture into your chosen Jello shot containers. Refrigerate for 4 hours or until firm. Makes 8-10 2oz Jello shots.

GIN

Nuclear Meltdown

6 oz pkg Pineapple Jello (or two 3 oz packages)
1 1/2 cups boiling water
½ cup cold water
¼ cup GIN
¼ cup TRIPLE SEC
½ cup VODKA
½ cup RUM
½ cup TEQUILA

Mix Gelatin with hot water until dissolved (approx 2 minutes). Add cold water, stir. Let sit until steam dissipates (no more than three minutes). Add Alcohol, Stir thoroughly (1-2 minutes). Pour mixture into your chosen Jello shot containers. Refrigerate for 4 hours or until firm. Makes 16-20 2oz Jello shots.

Grass Skirt

3 oz pkg Pineapple Jello
1 cup boiling water
½ cup cold water
splash of Grenadine
¼ cup GIN
¼ cup TRIPLE SEC

Mix Gelatin with hot water until dissolved (approx 2 minutes). Add cold water, splash of grenadine, and stir. Let sit until steam dissipates (no more than three minutes). Add Alcohol, Stir thoroughly (1-2 minutes). Pour mixture into your chosen Jello shot containers. Refrigerate for 4 hours or until firm. Makes 8-10 2oz Jello shots.

Little Devil

3 oz pkg Lemon Jello
¾ cup boiling water
¼ cup cold water
1/3 cup GIN
1/3 cup RUM
1/3 cup TRIPLE SEC

Mix Gelatin with hot water until dissolved (approx 2 minutes). Add cold water, stir. Let sit until steam dissipates (no more than three minutes). Add Alcohol, Stir thoroughly (1-2 minutes). Pour mixture into your chosen Jello shot containers. Refrigerate for 4 hours or until firm. Makes 8-10 2oz Jello shots.

GIN

Loud Speaker

3 oz pkg Lemon Jello
¾ cup boiling water
¼ cup cold water
1/3 cup GIN
1/3 cup BRANDY
1/3 cup ORANGE LIQUEUR

Mix Gelatin with hot water until dissolved (approx 2 minutes). Add cold water, stir. Let sit until steam dissipates (no more than three minutes). Add Alcohol, Stir thoroughly (1-2 minutes). Pour mixture into your chosen Jello shot containers. Refrigerate for 4 hours or until firm. Makes 8-10 2oz Jello shots.

Jack Daniels

Jack Daniels

Rebel Yell

3 oz pkg Peach Jello
1 cup boiling water
½ cup cold water
½ cup JACK DANIELS

Mix Gelatin with hot water until dissolved (approx 2 minutes). Add cold water, stir. Let sit until steam dissipates (no more than three minutes). Add Alcohol, Stir thoroughly (1-2 minutes). Pour mixture into your chosen Jello shot containers. Refrigerate for 4 hours or until firm. Makes 8-10 2oz Jello shots.

Yellow Jacket

3 oz pkg Orange Jello
1 cup boiling water
½ cup cold water
½ cup JACK DANIELS

Mix Gelatin with hot water until dissolved (approx 2 minutes). Add cold water, stir. Let sit until steam dissipates (no more than three minutes). Add Alcohol, Stir thoroughly (1-2 minutes). Pour mixture into your chosen Jello shot containers. Refrigerate for 4 hours or until firm. Makes 8-10 2oz Jello shots

Jagermeister

Jagermeister

Cough Drop

3 oz pkg Strawberry Jello
1 cup boiling water
½ cup cold water
½ cup JAGERMEISTER

Mix Gelatin with hot water until dissolved (approx 2 minutes). Add cold water, stir. Let sit until steam dissipates (no more than three minutes). Add Alcohol, Stir thoroughly (1-2 minutes). Pour mixture into your chosen Jello shot containers. Refrigerate for 4 hours or until firm. Makes 8-10 2oz Jello shots.

Crazy Red Head

3 oz pkg Cranberry Jello
1 cup boiling water
½ cup cold water
¼ cup JAGERMEISTER
¼ cup PEACH SCHNAPPS

Mix Gelatin with hot water until dissolved (approx 2 minutes). Add cold water, stir. Let sit until steam dissipates (no more than three minutes). Add Alcohol, Stir thoroughly (1-2 minutes). Pour mixture into your chosen Jello shot containers. Refrigerate for 4 hours or until firm. Makes 8-10 2oz Jello shots.

Jager-Master

3 oz pkg Orange Jello
1 cup boiling water
½ cup cold water
splash of Grenadine
¼ cup AMARETTO
¼ cup JAGERMEISTER

Mix Gelatin with hot water until dissolved (approx 2 minutes). Add cold water, stir. Let sit until steam dissipates (no more than three minutes). Add Alcohol, Stir thoroughly (1-2 minutes). Pour mixture into your chosen Jello shot containers. Refrigerate for 4 hours or until firm. Makes 8-10 2oz Jello shots.

Liqueur(s)

Liqueur(s)

Chocolate Covered Cherry

3 oz pkg Cherry Jello (or black cherry)
1 cup boiling water
½ cup cold water
¼ cup CHOCOLATE LIQUEUR
¼ cup VODKA

Mix Gelatin with hot water until dissolved (approx 2 minutes). Add cold water, stir. Let sit until steam dissipates (no more than three minutes). Add Alcohol, Stir thoroughly (1-2 minutes). Pour mixture into your chosen Jello shot containers. Refrigerate for 4 hours or until firm. Makes 8-10 2oz Jello shots.

Broken Heart

3 oz pkg Orange Jello
1 cup boiling water
½ cup cold water
¼ cup VODKA
¼ cup BLACK RASPBERRY LIQUEUR

Mix Gelatin with hot water until dissolved (approx 2 minutes). Add cold water, stir. Let sit until steam dissipates (no more than three minutes). Add Alcohol, Stir thoroughly (1-2 minutes). Pour mixture into your chosen Jello shot containers. Refrigerate for 4 hours or until firm. Makes 8-10 2oz Jello shots.

G-spot

3 oz pkg Cranberry Jello
1 cup boiling water
½ cup cold water
¼ cup VODKA
¼ cup ORANGE LIQUEUR

Mix Gelatin with hot water until dissolved (approx 2 minutes). Add cold water, stir. Let sit until steam dissipates (no more than three minutes). Add Alcohol, Stir thoroughly (1-2 minutes). Pour mixture into your chosen Jello shot containers. Refrigerate for 4 hours or until firm. Makes 8-10 2oz Jello shots.

Liqueur(s)

Juicy Fruit

3 oz pkg Pineapple Jello
¾ cup boiling water
¼ cup cold water
1/3 cup VODKA
1/3 cup PEACH SCHNAPPS
1/3 cup MELON LIQUEUR

Mix Gelatin with hot water until dissolved (approx 2 minutes). Add cold water, stir. Let sit until steam dissipates (no more than three minutes). Add Alcohol, Stir thoroughly (1-2 minutes). Pour mixture into your chosen Jello shot containers. Refrigerate for 4 hours or until firm. Makes 8-10 2oz Jello shots.

Purple Haze

3 oz pkg Cranberry Jello
1 cup boiling water
½ cup cold water
¼ cup VODKA
¼ cup BLACK RASPBERRY LIQUEUR

Mix Gelatin with hot water until dissolved (approx 2 minutes). Add cold water, stir. Let sit until steam dissipates (no more than three minutes). Add Alcohol, Stir thoroughly (1-2 minutes). Pour mixture into your chosen Jello shot containers. Refrigerate for 4 hours or until firm. Makes 8-10 2oz Jello shots.

Bomb Pop

3 oz pkg Lemon Jello
3/4 cup boiling water
½ cup cold water
½ cup RASPBERRY VODKA
¼ cup BLUE CURACOA

Mix Gelatin with hot water until dissolved (approx 2 minutes). Add cold water, stir. Let sit until steam dissipates (no more than three minutes). Add Alcohol, Stir thoroughly (1-2 minutes). Pour mixture into your chosen Jello shot containers. Refrigerate for 4 hours or until firm. Makes 8-10 2oz Jello shots.

Liqueur(s)

Bat out of Hell

3 z pkg Orange Jello
1 cup boiling water
½ cup Red Bull (energy Drink)
¼ cup RUM
¼ cup BLUE CURACOA

Mix Gelatin with hot water until dissolved (approx 2 minutes). Add RED BULL, stir. Let sit until steam dissipates (no more than three minutes). Add Alcohol, Stir thoroughly (1-2 minutes). Pour mixture into your chosen Jello shot containers. Refrigerate for 4 hours or until firm. Makes 8-10 2oz Jello shots.

Busted Rubber

3 oz pkg Orange Jello
1 cup boiling water
½ cup cold water
¼ cup RASPBERRY LIQUEUR
¼ cup IRISH CREAM

Mix Gelatin with hot water until dissolved (approx 2 minutes). Add cold water, stir. Let sit until steam dissipates (no more than three minutes). Add Alcohol, Stir thoroughly (1-2 minutes). Pour mixture into your chosen Jello shot containers. Refrigerate for 4 hours or until firm. Makes 8-10 2oz Jello shots.

Pain Killer

3 oz pkg Pineapple Jello
¾ cup boiling water
¼ cup cold water
1/3 cup DARK RUM
1/3 cup COCONUT RUM
1/3 cup ORANGE LIQUEUR

Mix Gelatin with hot water until dissolved (approx 2 minutes). Add cold water, stir. Let sit until steam dissipates (no more than three minutes). Add Alcohol, Stir thoroughly (1-2 minutes). Pour mixture into your chosen Jello shot containers. Refrigerate for 4 hours or until firm. Makes 8-10 2oz Jello shots.

Liqueur(s)

Mockingbird

3 oz pkg Lime Jello
1 cup boiling water
½ cup cold water
¼ cup TEQUILA
¼ cup CRÈME DE MENTHE (white)

Mix Gelatin with hot water until dissolved (approx 2 minutes). Add cold water, stir. Let sit until steam dissipates (no more than three minutes). Add Alcohol, Stir thoroughly (1-2 minutes). Pour mixture into your chosen Jello shot containers. Refrigerate for 4 hours or until firm. Makes 8-10 2oz Jello shots.

Kiwi Kiss

3 oz pkg Orange Jello
1 cup boiling water
½ cup cold water
¼ cup BANANA LIQUEUR
¼ cup STRAWBERRY LIQUEUR

Mix Gelatin with hot water until dissolved (approx 2 minutes). Add cold water, stir. Let sit until steam dissipates (no more than three minutes). Add Alcohol, Stir thoroughly (1-2 minutes). Pour mixture into your chosen Jello shot containers. Refrigerate for 4 hours or until firm. Makes 8-10 2oz Jello shots.

Piñata

3 oz pkg Lime Jello
1 cup boiling water
½ cup cold water
¼ cup TEQUILA
¼ cup BANANA LIQUEUR

Mix Gelatin with hot water until dissolved (approx 2 minutes). Add cold water, stir. Let sit until steam dissipates (no more than three minutes). Add Alcohol, Stir thoroughly (1-2 minutes). Pour mixture into your chosen Jello shot containers. Refrigerate for 4 hours or until firm. Makes 8-10 2oz Jello shots.

Liqueur(s)

Killer Whale

3 oz pkg Cranberry Jello
3 oz pkg Orange Jello
2 cups boiling water
1 cup cold water
¼ cup VODKA
¼ cup RUM
¼ cup BLACK RASPBERRY LIQUEUR
¼ cup TRIPLE SEC

Mix Gelatin with hot water until dissolved (approx 2 minutes). Add cold water, stir. Let sit until steam dissipates (no more than three minutes). Add Alcohol, Stir thoroughly (1-2 minutes). Pour mixture into your chosen Jello shot containers. Refrigerate for 4 hours or until firm. Makes 16-20 2oz Jello shots

Banana Split

3 oz pkg Strawberry Jello
1 cup boiling water
¼ cup cold water
¼ cup VODKA
¼ cup BANANA LIQUEUR
¼ cup CRÈME DE CACAO

Mix Gelatin with hot water until dissolved (approx 2 minutes). Add cold water, stir. Let sit until steam dissipates (no more than three minutes). Add Alcohol, Stir thoroughly (1-2 minutes). Pour mixture into your chosen Jello shot containers. Refrigerate for 4 hours or until firm. Makes 8-10 2oz Jello shots.

Bitch Fight

3 oz pkg Cranberry Jello
1 cup boiling water
¼ cup cold water
¼ cup lime juice
¼ cup PEACH SCHNAPPS
¼ cup ORANGE LIQUEUR

Mix Gelatin with hot water until dissolved (approx 2 minutes). Add cold water, and lime juice. Stir. Let sit until steam dissipates (no more than three minutes). Add Alcohol, Stir thoroughly (1-2 minutes). Pour mixture into your chosen Jello shot containers. Refrigerate for 4 hours or until firm. Makes 8-10 2oz Jello shots.

Liqueur(s)

Loud Speaker

3 oz pkg Lemon Jello
¾ cup boiling water
¼ cup cold water
1/3 cup GIN
1/3 cup BRANDY
1/3 cup ORANGE LIQUEUR

Mix Gelatin with hot water until dissolved (approx 2 minutes). Add cold water, stir. Let sit until steam dissipates (no more than three minutes). Add Alcohol, Stir thoroughly (1-2 minutes). Pour mixture into your chosen Jello shot containers. Refrigerate for 4 hours or until firm. Makes 8-10 2oz Jello shots.

Mac Daddy

3 oz pkg Pineapple Jello
1 cup boiling water
½ cup cold water
¼ cup GIN
¼ cup CHERRY LIQUEUR

Mix Gelatin with hot water until dissolved (approx 2 minutes). Add cold water, stir. Let sit until steam dissipates (no more than three minutes). Add Alcohol, Stir thoroughly (1-2 minutes). Pour mixture into your chosen Jello shot containers. Refrigerate for 4 hours or until firm. Makes 8-10 2oz Jello shots.

PB&J

3 oz pkg Raspberry Jello
1 cup boiling water
½ cup cold water
¼ cup HAZELNUT LIQUEUR
¼ cup BLACK RASPBERRY LIQUEUR

Mix Gelatin with hot water until dissolved (approx 2 minutes). Add cold water, stir. Let sit until steam dissipates (no more than three minutes). Add Alcohol, Stir thoroughly (1-2 minutes). Pour mixture into your chosen Jello shot containers. Refrigerate for 4 hours or until firm. Makes 8-10 2oz Jello shots.

Liqueur(s)

Pez

3 oz pkg Lemon Jello
1 cup boiling water
½ cup cold water
¼ cup SPICED RUM
¼ cup BLACK RASPBERRY LIQUEUR

Mix Gelatin with hot water until dissolved (approx 2 minutes). Add cold water, stir. Let sit until steam dissipates (no more than three minutes). Add Alcohol, Stir thoroughly (1-2 minutes). Pour mixture into your chosen Jello shot containers. Refrigerate for 4 hours or until firm. Makes 8-10 2oz Jello shots.

Scooby Snack

3 oz pkg Pineapple Jello
1 cup boiling water
½ cup cold water
¼ cup melon liqueur
¼ cup coconut rum

Mix Gelatin with hot water until dissolved (approx 2 minutes). Add cold water, stir. Let sit until steam dissipates (no more than three minutes). Add Alcohol, Stir thoroughly (1-2 minutes). Pour mixture into your chosen Jello shot containers. Refrigerate for 4 hours or until firm. Makes 8-10 2oz Jello shots.

Killer Koolaide

6 oz pkg Cranberry Jello (or two 3 oz packages)
1 ½ cups boiling water
¾ cup cold water
½ cup VODKA
½ cup GIN
¼ cup RUM
¼ cup CHAMBORG
¼ cup TRIPLE SEC

Mix Gelatin with hot water until dissolved (approx 2 minutes). Add cold water, stir. Let sit until steam dissipates (no more than three minutes). Add Alcohol, Stir thoroughly (1-2 minutes). Pour mixture into your chosen Jello shot containers. Refrigerate for 4 hours or until firm. Makes 16-20 2oz Jello shots.

Liqueur(s)

Leisure Suit

3 oz pkg Orange Jello
3 oz pkg Cranberry Jello
3 oz pkg Pineapple Jello
3 cups boiling water
1½ cups cold water
¾ cup BANANA LIQUEUR
¾ cup GALLIANO

Mix Gelatin with hot water until dissolved (approx 2 minutes). Add cold water, stir. Let sit until steam dissipates (no more than three minutes). Add Alcohol, Stir thoroughly (1-2 minutes). Pour mixture into your chosen Jello shot containers. Refrigerate for 4 hours or until firm. Makes 24-30 2oz Jello shots.

Banana Boat

3 oz pkg Pineapple Jello
1 cup boiling water
½ cup cold water
¼ cup COCONUT RUM
¼ cup BANANA LIQUEUR

Mix Gelatin with hot water until dissolved (approx 2 minutes). Add cold water, stir. Let sit until steam dissipates (no more than three minutes). Add Alcohol, Stir thoroughly (1-2 minutes). Pour mixture into your chosen Jello shot containers. Refrigerate for 4 hours or until firm. Makes 8-10 2oz Jello shots.

Purple Mask

3 oz pkg Grape Jello
1 cup boiling water
¼ cup cold water
½ cup VODKA
¼ cup CRÈME DE COCOA (white)

Mix Gelatin with hot water until dissolved (approx 2 minutes). Add cold water, stir. Let sit until steam dissipates (no more than three minutes). Add Alcohol, Stir thoroughly (1-2 minutes). Pour mixture into your chosen Jello shot containers. Refrigerate for 4 hours or until firm. Makes 8-10 2oz Jello shots.

Liqueur(s)

Robins Nest

3 oz pkg Cranberry Jello
1 cup boiling water
¼ cup cold water
½ cup VODKA
¼ cup CRÈME DE COCOA (white)

Mix Gelatin with hot water until dissolved (approx 2 minutes). Add cold water, stir. Let sit until steam dissipates (no more than three minutes). Add Alcohol, Stir thoroughly (1-2 minutes). Pour mixture into your chosen Jello shot containers. Refrigerate for 4 hours or until firm. Makes 8-10 2oz Jello shots.

Top Banana

3 oz pkg Orange Jello
1 cup boiling water
¼ cup cold water
½ cup VODKA
¼ cup CRÈME DE BANANA

Mix Gelatin with hot water until dissolved (approx 2 minutes). Add cold water, stir. Let sit until steam dissipates (no more than three minutes). Add Alcohol, Stir thoroughly (1-2 minutes). Pour mixture into your chosen Jello shot containers. Refrigerate for 4 hours or until firm. Makes 8-10 2oz Jello shots.

Smooth –n- Easy

3 oz pkg Strawberry Jello
1 cup boiling water
¼ cup cold water
½ cup VODKA
¼ cup CRÈME DE BANANA

Mix Gelatin with hot water until dissolved (approx 2 minutes). Add cold water, stir. Let sit until steam dissipates (no more than three minutes). Add Alcohol, Stir thoroughly (1-2 minutes). Pour mixture into your chosen Jello shot containers. Refrigerate for 4 hours or until firm. Makes 8-10 2oz Jello shots.

Liqueur(s)

Parrot Head

3 oz pkg Pineapple Jello
1 cup boiling water
½ cup cold water
¼ cup SPICED RUM
¼ cup BLACK RASPBERRY LIQUEUR

Mix Gelatin with hot water until dissolved (approx 2 minutes). Add cold water, stir. Let sit until steam dissipates (no more than three minutes). Add Alcohol, Stir thoroughly (1-2 minutes). Pour mixture into your chosen Jello shot containers. Refrigerate for 4 hours or until firm. Makes 8-10 2oz Jello shots.

Strawberry Kick

3 oz pkg Strawberry Jello
1 cup boiling water
¼ cup cold water
¼ cup STRAWBERRY LIQUEUR
½ cup LIGHT RUM

Mix Gelatin with hot water until dissolved (approx 2 minutes). Add cold water, stir. Let sit until steam dissipates (no more than three minutes). Add Alcohol, Stir thoroughly (1-2 minutes). Pour mixture into your chosen Jello shot containers. Refrigerate for 4 hours or until firm. Makes 8-10 2oz Jello shots.

Green Devil

3 oz pkg Lime Jello
1 cup boiling water
½ cup cold water
¼ cup GIN
¼ cup CRÈME DE MENTHE

Mix Gelatin with hot water until dissolved (approx 2 minutes). Add cold water, stir. Let sit until steam dissipates (no more than three minutes). Add Alcohol, Stir thoroughly (1-2 minutes). Pour mixture into your chosen Jello shot containers. Refrigerate for 4 hours or until firm. Makes 8-10 2oz Jello shots.

Liqueur(s)

Miami Breeze

3 oz pkg Lemon Jello
1 cup boiling water
¼ cup cold water
½ cup LIGHT RUM
¼ cup CRÈME DE MENTHE (white)

Mix Gelatin with hot water until dissolved (approx 2 minutes). Add cold water, stir. Let sit until steam dissipates (no more than three minutes). Add Alcohol, Stir thoroughly (1-2 minutes). Pour mixture into your chosen Jello shot containers. Refrigerate for 4 hours or until firm. Makes 8-10 2oz Jello shots.

Purple Hooter

3 oz pkg Lime Jello
1 cup boiling water
½ cup cold water
¼ cup VODKA
¼ cup BLACK RASPBERRY LIQUEUR

Mix Gelatin with hot water until dissolved (approx 2 minutes). Add cold water, stir. Let sit until steam dissipates (no more than three minutes). Add Alcohol, Stir thoroughly (1-2 minutes). Pour mixture into your chosen Jello shot containers. Refrigerate for 4 hours or until firm. Makes 8-10 2oz Jello shots.

Moon Racker

3 oz pkg Pineapple Jello
1 cup boiling water
½ cup cold water
¼ cup TEQUILA
¼ cup BLUE CURACOA

Mix Gelatin with hot water until dissolved (approx 2 minutes). Add cold water, stir. Let sit until steam dissipates (no more than three minutes). Add Alcohol, Stir thoroughly (1-2 minutes). Pour mixture into your chosen Jello shot containers. Refrigerate for 4 hours or until firm. Makes 8-10 2oz Jello shots.

Liqueur(s)

Ninja Turtle

3 oz pkg Orange Jello
1 cup boiling water
½ cup cold water
¼ cup GIN
¼ cup BLUE CURACOA

Mix Gelatin with hot water until dissolved (approx 2 minutes). Add cold water, stir. Let sit until steam dissipates (no more than three minutes). Add Alcohol, Stir thoroughly (1-2 minutes). Pour mixture into your chosen Jello shot containers. Refrigerate for 4 hours or until firm. Makes 8-10 2oz Jello shots.

Leprechaun

3 oz orange Jello
¾ cup boiling water
¼ cup cold water
1/3 cup PEACH SCHNAPPS
1/3 cup PEACH VODKA
1/3 cup BLUE CURACOA

Mix Gelatin with hot water until dissolved (approx 2 minutes). Add cold water, stir. Let sit until steam dissipates (no more than three minutes). Add Alcohol, Stir thoroughly (1-2 minutes). Pour mixture into your chosen Jello shot containers. Refrigerate for 4 hours or until firm. Makes 8-10 2oz Jello shots.

Life Savor

3 oz pkg Orange Jello
¾ cup boiling water
¼ cup cold water
1/3 cup TRIPLE SEC
1/3 cup MELON LIQUEUR
1/3 cup COCONUT RUM

Mix Gelatin with hot water until dissolved (approx 2 minutes). Add cold water, stir. Let sit until steam dissipates (no more than three minutes). Add Alcohol, Stir thoroughly (1-2 minutes). Pour mixture into your chosen Jello shot containers. Refrigerate for 4 hours or until firm. Makes 8-10 2oz Jello shots.

Liqueur(s)

Blue Hawaiian

3 oz pkg Pineapple Jello
¾ cup boiling water
½ cup cold water
¼ cup BLUE CURACOA
¼ cup COCONUT RUM
¼ cup LIGHT RUM

Mix Gelatin with hot water until dissolved (approx 2 minutes). Add cold water, stir. Let sit until steam dissipates (no more than three minutes). Add Alcohol, Stir thoroughly (1-2 minutes). Pour mixture into your chosen Jello shot containers. Refrigerate for 4 hours or until firm. Makes 8-10 2oz Jello shots.

Tijuana Taxi

6 oz pkg Lemon Jello (or two 3 oz packages)
2 cups boiling water
1 cup cold water
½ cup TEQUILA
¼ cup BLUE CURACOU
¼ cup TROPICAL FRUIT SCHNAPPS

Mix Gelatin with hot water until dissolved (approx 2 minutes). Add cold water, stir. Let sit until steam dissipates (no more than three minutes). Add Alcohol, Stir thoroughly (1-2 minutes). Pour mixture into your chosen Jello shot containers. Refrigerate for 4 hours or until firm. Makes 16-20 2oz Jello shots.

Blue Lagoon

3 oz pkg Lemon Jello
1 cup boiling water
¼ cup cold water
½ cup VODKA
¼ cup BLUE CURACOA

Mix Gelatin with hot water until dissolved (approx 2 minutes). Add cold water, stir. Let sit until steam dissipates (no more than three minutes). Add Alcohol, Stir thoroughly (1-2 minutes). Pour mixture into your chosen Jello shot containers. Refrigerate for 4 hours or until firm. Makes 8-10 2oz Jello shots.

Liqueur(s)

Pineapple Upside Down Cake

3 oz pkg pineapple Jello
¾ cup boiling water
¼ cup cold water
½ cup VODKA
¼ cup IRISH CRÈME
¼ cup BUTTERSCOTCH SCHNAPPS

Mix Gelatin with hot water until dissolved (approx 2 minutes). Add cold water, stir. Let sit until steam dissipates (no more than three minutes). Add Alcohol, Stir thoroughly (1-2 minutes). Pour mixture into your chosen Jello shot containers. Refrigerate for 4 hours or until firm. Makes 8-10 2oz Jello shots.

Adam and Eve

3 oz pkg Lemon Jello
¾ cup boiling water
½ cup cold water
¼ cup BRANDY
¼ cup FORBIDDEN FRUIT LIQUEUR
¼ cup GIN

Mix Gelatin with hot water until dissolved (approx 2 minutes). Add cold water, stir. Let sit until steam dissipates (no more than three minutes). Add Alcohol, Stir thoroughly (1-2 minutes). Pour mixture into your chosen Jello shot containers. Refrigerate for 4 hours or until firm. Makes 8-10 2oz Jello shots.

Naked Pretzel

3 oz pkg Pineapple Jello
¾ cup boiling water
¼ cup cold water
½ cup VODKA
¼ cup MELON LIQUEUR
¼ cup CRÈME DE CASSIS

Mix Gelatin with hot water until dissolved (approx 2 minutes). Add cold water, stir. Let sit until steam dissipates (no more than three minutes). Add Alcohol, Stir thoroughly (1-2 minutes). Pour mixture into your chosen Jello shot containers. Refrigerate for 4 hours or until firm. Makes 8-10 2oz Jello shots.

Liqueur(s)

Rain Man

3 oz pkg Orange Jello
1 cup boiling water
¼ cup cold water
½ cup 151 RUM
¼ cup MELON LIQUEUR

Mix Gelatin with hot water until dissolved (approx 2 minutes). Add cold water, stir. Let sit until steam dissipates (no more than three minutes). Add Alcohol, Stir thoroughly (1-2 minutes). Pour mixture into your chosen Jello shot containers. Refrigerate for 4 hours or until firm. Makes 8-10 2oz Jello shots.

Melon Ball

3 oz pkg Pineapple Jello
1 cup boiling water
¼ cup cold water
½ cup VODKA
¼ Melon LIQUEUR

Mix Gelatin with hot water until dissolved (approx 2 minutes). Add cold water, stir. Let sit until steam dissipates (no more than three minutes). Add Alcohol, Stir thoroughly (1-2 minutes). Pour mixture into your chosen Jello shot containers. Refrigerate for 4 hours or until firm. Makes 8-10 2oz Jello shots.

June Bug

3 oz pkg Pineapple Jello
3 oz pkg Cranberry Jello
2 cups boiling water
1 cup cold water
1/3 cup BANANA LIQUEUR
1/3 cup MELON LIQUEUR
1/3 cup PEACH SCHNAPPS

Mix Gelatin with hot water until dissolved (approx 2 minutes). Add cold water, stir. Let sit until steam dissipates (no more than three minutes). Add Alcohol, Stir thoroughly (1-2 minutes). Pour mixture into your chosen Jello shot containers. Refrigerate for 4 hours or until firm. Makes 16-20 2oz Jello shots.

<u>Liqueur(s)</u>

Melon Cooler

6 oz pkg Pineapple Jello (two 3 oz packages)
2 cups boiling water
1 cup cold water
½ cup MELON LIQUEUR
¼ cup PEACH SCHNAPPS
¼ cup RASPBERRY SCHNAPPS

Mix Gelatin with hot water until dissolved (approx 2 minutes). Add cold water, stir. Let sit until steam dissipates (no more than three minutes). Add Alcohol, Stir thoroughly (1-2 minutes). Pour mixture into your chosen Jello shot containers. Refrigerate for 4 hours or until firm. Makes 8-10 2oz Jello shots.

Grand Marnier

3 oz pkg Orange Jello
1 cup boiling water
½ cup cold water
¼ cup BRANDY
¼ cup ORANGE COGNAC

Mix Gelatin with hot water until dissolved (approx 2 minutes). Add cold water, stir. Let sit until steam dissipates (no more than three minutes). Add Alcohol, Stir thoroughly (1-2 minutes). Pour mixture into your chosen Jello shot containers. Refrigerate for 4 hours or until firm. Makes 8-10 2oz Jello shots.

Ecstasy

3 oz pkg Pineapple Jello
3 oz pkg Cranberry Jello
2 cups boiling water
1 cup cold water
½ cup VODKA
½ cup BLACK RASPBERRY LIQUEUR

Mix Gelatin with hot water until dissolved (approx 2 minutes). Add cold water and cola, stir. Let sit until steam dissipates (no more than three minutes). Add Alcohol, Stir thoroughly (1-2 minutes). Pour mixture into your chosen Jello shot containers. Refrigerate for 4 hours or until firm. Makes 16-20 2oz Jello shots.

Liqueur(s)

Green Demon

3 oz pkg Lemon Jello
¾ cup boiling water
¼ cup cold water
1/3 cup VODKA
1/3 cup RUM
1/3 cup MELON LIQUEUR

Mix Gelatin with hot water until dissolved (approx 2 minutes). Add cold water, stir. Let sit until steam dissipates (no more than three minutes). Add Alcohol, Stir thoroughly (1-2 minutes). Pour mixture into your chosen Jello shot containers. Refrigerate for 4 hours or until firm. Makes 8-10 2oz Jello shots.

Pucker

Pucker

Jolly Rancher

3 oz pkg of your favorite Jello flavor
1 cup boiling water
½ cup cold water
½ cup of your favorite PUCKER LIQUEUR

Mix Gelatin with hot water until dissolved (approx 2 minutes). Add cold water, stir. Let sit until steam dissipates (no more than three minutes). Add Alcohol, Stir thoroughly (1-2 minutes). Pour mixture into your chosen Jello shot containers. Refrigerate for 4 hours or until firm. Makes 8-10 2oz Jello shots.

Green Apples

3 oz pkg Lime Jello
1 cup boiling water
½ cup cold water
½ cup APPLE PUCKER

Sprinkle with sugar before serving

Mix Gelatin with hot water until dissolved (approx 2 minutes). Add cold water, stir. Let sit until steam dissipates (no more than three minutes). Add Alcohol, Stir thoroughly (1-2 minutes). Pour mixture into your chosen Jello shot containers. Refrigerate for 4 hours or until firm. Makes 8-10 2oz Jello shots.

Sour Apple

3 oz pkg Lime Jello
¾ cup boiling water
½ cup cold water
½ cup VODKA
¼ cup APPLE PUCKERS

Mix Gelatin with hot water until dissolved (approx 2 minutes). Add cold water, stir. Let sit until steam dissipates (no more than three minutes). Add Alcohol, Stir thoroughly (1-2 minutes). Pour mixture into your chosen Jello shot containers. Refrigerate for 4 hours or until firm. Makes 8-10 2oz Jello shots.

Pucker

Apple Core

3 oz Green Apple Jello
1 cup boiling water
½ cup cold water
½ cup SOUR APPLE PUCKER

Mix Gelatin with hot water until dissolved (approx 2 minutes). Add cold water, stir. Let sit until steam dissipates (no more than three minutes). Add Alcohol, Stir thoroughly (1-2 minutes). Pour mixture into your chosen Jello shot containers. Refrigerate for 4 hours or until firm. Makes 8-10 2oz Jello shots.

Blue Islander

3 oz pkg Berry Blue Jello
1 cup boiling water
½ cup cold water
¼ cup VODKA
¼ cup ISLAND PUCKER

Mix Gelatin with hot water until dissolved (approx 2 minutes). Add cold water, stir. Let sit until steam dissipates (no more than three minutes). Add Alcohol, Stir thoroughly (1-2 minutes). Pour mixture into your chosen Jello shot containers. Refrigerate for 4 hours or until firm. Makes 8-10 2oz Jello shots.

RUM

<u>RUM</u>

Scooby Snack

3 oz pkg Pineapple Jello
1 cup boiling water
½ cup cold water
¼ cup MELON LIQUEUR
¼ cup COCONUT RUM

Mix Gelatin with hot water until dissolved (approx 2 minutes). Add cold water, stir. Let sit until steam dissipates (no more than three minutes). Add Alcohol, Stir thoroughly (1-2 minutes). Pour mixture into your chosen Jello shot containers. Refrigerate for 4 hours or until firm. Makes 8-10 2oz Jello shots.

Brass Monkey

3 oz pkg Orange Jello
1 cup boiling water
½ cup cold water
¼ cup RUM
¼ cup VODKA

Mix Gelatin with hot water until dissolved (approx 2 minutes). Add cold water, stir. Let sit until steam dissipates (no more than three minutes). Add Alcohol, Stir thoroughly (1-2 minutes). Pour mixture into your chosen Jello shot containers. Refrigerate for 4 hours or until firm. Makes 8-10 2oz Jello shots.

Green Demon

3 oz pkg Lemon Jello
¾ cup boiling water
¼ cup cold water
1/3 cup VODKA
1/3 cup RUM
1/3 cup MELON LIQUEUR

Mix Gelatin with hot water until dissolved (approx 2 minutes). Add cold water, stir. Let sit until steam dissipates (no more than three minutes). Add Alcohol, Stir thoroughly (1-2 minutes). Pour mixture into your chosen Jello shot containers. Refrigerate for 4 hours or until firm. Makes 8-10 2oz Jello shots.

RUM

Killer Whale

3 oz pkg Cranberry Jello
3 oz pkg Orange Jello
2 cups boiling water
1 cup cold water
¼ cup VODKA
¼ cup RUM
¼ cup BLACK RASPBERRY LIQUEUR
¼ cup TRIPLE SEC

Mix Gelatin with hot water until dissolved (approx 2 minutes). Add cold water, stir. Let sit until steam dissipates (no more than three minutes). Add Alcohol, Stir thoroughly (1-2 minutes). Pour mixture into your chosen Jello shot containers. Refrigerate for 4 hours or until firm. Makes 16-20 2oz Jello shots.

Ankle Breaker

3 oz pkg Lime Jello
1 cup boiling water
½ cup cold water
¼ cup 151 RUM
¼ cup CHERY BRANDY

Mix Gelatin with hot water until dissolved (approx 2 minutes). Add cold water, stir. Let sit until steam dissipates (no more than three minutes). Add Alcohol, Stir thoroughly (1-2 minutes). Pour mixture into your chosen Jello shot containers. Refrigerate for 4 hours or until firm. Makes 8-10 2oz Jello shots.

Bat out of Hell

3 z pkg Orange Jello
1 cup boiling water
½ cup Red Bull (energy Drink)
¼ cup RUM
¼ cup BLUE CURACOA

Mix Gelatin with hot water until dissolved (approx 2 minutes). Add RED BULL, stir. Let sit until steam dissipates (no more than three minutes). Add Alcohol, Stir thoroughly (1-2 minutes). Pour mixture into your chosen Jello shot containers. Refrigerate for 4 hours or until firm. Makes 8-10 2oz Jello shots.

RUM

Nuclear Meltdown

6 oz pkg Pineapple Jello (or two 3 oz packages)
1 1/2 cups boiling water
½ cup cold water
¼ cup GIN
¼ cup TRIPLE SEC
½ cup VODKA
½ cup RUM
½ cup TEQUILA

Mix Gelatin with hot water until dissolved (approx 2 minutes). Add cold water, stir. Let sit until steam dissipates (no more than three minutes). Add Alcohol, Stir thoroughly (1-2 minutes). Pour mixture into your chosen Jello shot containers. Refrigerate for 4 hours or until firm. Makes 16-20 2oz Jello shots.

Bermuda Triangle

3 oz pkg Orange Jello
1 cup boiling water
½ cup cld water
¼ cup SPICED RUM
¼ cup PEACH SCHNAPPS

Mix Gelatin with hot water until dissolved (approx 2 minutes). Add cold water, stir. Let sit until steam dissipates (no more than three minutes). Add Alcohol, Stir thoroughly (1-2 minutes). Pour mixture into your chosen Jello shot containers. Refrigerate for 4 hours or until firm. Makes 8-10 2oz Jello shots.

Banana Boat

3 oz pkg Pineapple Jello
1 cup boiling water
½ cup cold water
¼ cup COCONUT RUM
¼ cup BANANA LIQUEUR

Mix Gelatin with hot water until dissolved (approx 2 minutes). Add cold water, stir. Let sit until steam dissipates (no more than three minutes). Add Alcohol, Stir thoroughly (1-2 minutes). Pour mixture into your chosen Jello shot containers. Refrigerate for 4 hours or until firm. Makes 8-10 2oz Jello shots.

RUM

Miami Breeze

3 oz pkg Lemon Jello
1 cup boiling water
¼ cup cold water
½ cup LIGHT RUM
¼ cup CRÈME DE MENTHE (white)

Mix Gelatin with hot water until dissolved (approx 2 minutes). Add cold water, stir. Let sit until steam dissipates (no more than three minutes). Add Alcohol, Stir thoroughly (1-2 minutes). Pour mixture into your chosen Jello shot containers. Refrigerate for 4 hours or until firm. Makes 8-10 2oz Jello shots.

Chi-Chi

3 oz pkg Pineapple Jello
1 cup boiling water
½ cup cold water
¼ cup BLACKBERRY BRANDY
¼ cup RUM

Mix Gelatin with hot water until dissolved (approx 2 minutes). Add cold water, stir. Let sit until steam dissipates (no more than three minutes). Add Alcohol, Stir thoroughly (1-2 minutes). Pour mixture into your chosen Jello shot containers. Refrigerate for 4 hours or until firm. Makes 8-10 2oz Jello shots.

Rum Screwdriver

3 oz pkg Orange Jello
1 cup boiling water
½ cup cold water
½ cup LIGHT RUM

Mix Gelatin with hot water until dissolved (approx 2 minutes). Add cold water, stir. Let sit until steam dissipates (no more than three minutes). Add Alcohol, Stir thoroughly (1-2 minutes). Pour mixture into your chosen Jello shot containers. Refrigerate for 4 hours or until firm. Makes 8-10 2oz Jello shots.

RUM

Lethal Injection

3 oz pkg Orange Jello
3 oz pkg Pineapple Jello
2 cups boiling water
1 cup cold water
¼ cup AMARETTO
¼ cup DARK RUM
¼ cup SPICED RUM
¼ cup COCONUT RUM

Mix Gelatin with hot water until dissolved (approx 2 minutes). Add cold water, stir. Let sit until steam dissipates (no more than three minutes). Add Alcohol, Stir thoroughly (1-2 minutes). Pour mixture into your chosen Jello shot containers. Refrigerate for 4 hours or until firm. Makes 16-20 2oz Jello shots.

Firecracker

3 oz pkg Orange Jello
¾ cup boiling water
¼ cup cold water
1/3 cup SPICED RUM
1/3 cup SLOE GIN
1/3 cup 151 RUM

Mix Gelatin with hot water until dissolved (approx 2 minutes). Add cold water, stir. Let sit until steam dissipates (no more than three minutes). Add Alcohol, Stir thoroughly (1-2 minutes). Pour mixture into your chosen Jello shot containers. Refrigerate for 4 hours or until firm. Makes 8-10 2oz Jello shots.

Life Savor

3 oz pkg Orange Jello
¾ cup boiling water
¼ cup cold water
1/3 cup TRIPLE SEC
1/3 cup MELON LIQUEUR
1/3 cup COCONUT RUM

Mix Gelatin with hot water until dissolved (approx 2 minutes). Add cold water, stir. Let sit until steam dissipates (no more than three minutes). Add Alcohol, Stir thoroughly (1-2 minutes). Pour mixture into your chosen Jello shot containers. Refrigerate for 4 hours or until firm. Makes 8-10 2oz Jello shots.

RUM

Blue Hawaiian

3 oz pkg Pineapple Jello
¾ cup boiling water
½ cup cold water
¼ cup BLUE CURACOA
¼ cup COCONUT RUM
¼ cup LIGHT RUM

Mix Gelatin with hot water until dissolved (approx 2 minutes). Add cold water, stir. Let sit until steam dissipates (no more than three minutes). Add Alcohol, Stir thoroughly (1-2 minutes). Pour mixture into your chosen Jello shot containers. Refrigerate for 4 hours or until firm. Makes 8-10 2oz Jello shots.

Boston Sidecar

3 oz pkg Lime Jello
1 cup boiling water
¼ cup cold water
¼ cup BRANDY
¼ cup LIGHT RUM
¼ cup TRIPLE SEC

Mix Gelatin with hot water until dissolved (approx 2 minutes). Add cold water, stir. Let sit until steam dissipates (no more than three minutes). Add Alcohol, Stir thoroughly (1-2 minutes). Pour mixture into your chosen Jello shot containers. Refrigerate for 4 hours or until firm. Makes 8-10 2oz Jello shots.

Komaniwanalaya

3 oz pkg Pineapple Jello
3 oz pkg Cranberry Jello
2 cups boiling water
1 cup cold water
½ cup AMARETTO
½ cup 151 RUM

Mix Gelatin with hot water until dissolved (approx 2 minutes). Add cold water, stir. Let sit until steam dissipates (no more than three minutes). Add Alcohol, Stir thoroughly (1-2 minutes). Pour mixture into your chosen Jello shot containers. Refrigerate for 4 hours or until firm. Makes 16-20 2oz Jello shots.

RUM

Between the Sheets

3 oz pkg Lemon Jello
¾ cup boiling water
½ cup cold water
¼ cup BRANDY
¼ cup TRIPLE SEC
¼ cup LIGHT RUM

Mix Gelatin with hot water until dissolved (approx 2 minutes). Add cold water, stir. Let sit until steam dissipates (no more than three minutes). Add Alcohol, Stir thoroughly (1-2 minutes). Pour mixture into your chosen Jello shot containers. Refrigerate for 4 hours or until firm. Makes 8-10 2oz Jello shots.

Long Island Iced Tea

6 oz pkg Lemon Jello (or two 3 oz packages)
1 cup boiling water
½ cup cola
½ cup cold water
½ cup GIN
½ cup LIGHT RUM
½ cup VODKA
½ cup TEQUILA

Mix Gelatin with hot water until dissolved (approx 2 minutes). Add cold water and cola, stir. Let sit until steam dissipates (no more than three minutes). Add Alcohol, Stir thoroughly (1-2 minutes). Pour mixture into your chosen Jello shot containers. Refrigerate for 4 hours or until firm. Makes 8-10 2oz Jello shots.

Strawberry Kick

3 oz pkg Strawberry Jello
1 cup boiling water
¼ cup cold water
¼ cup STRAWBERRY LIQUEUR
½ cup LIGHT RUM

Mix Gelatin with hot water until dissolved (approx 2 minutes). Add cold water, stir. Let sit until steam dissipates (no more than three minutes). Add Alcohol, Stir thoroughly (1-2 minutes). Pour mixture into your chosen Jello shot containers. Refrigerate for 4 hours or until firm. Makes 8-10 2oz Jello shots.

RUM

Apple Pie

6 oz pkg Lemon Jello (or two 3 oz packages)
1 ½ cup boiling water
1 cup cold water
½ cup LIGHT RUM
½ cup SWEET VERMOUTH
¼ cup APPLE BRANDY
¼ cup Grenadine

Mix Gelatin with hot water until dissolved (approx 2 minutes). Add cold water, stir. Let sit until steam dissipates (no more than three minutes). Add grenadine and Alcohol, Stir thoroughly (1-2 minutes). Pour mixture into your chosen Jello shot containers. Refrigerate for 4 hours or until firm. Makes 16-20 2oz Jello shots.

Strawberry Daiquiri

3 oz pkg Strawberry Daiquiri Jello
1 cup boiling water
½ cup cold water
½ cup RUM

Mix Gelatin with hot water until dissolved (approx 2 minutes). Add cold water, stir. Let sit until steam dissipates (no more than three minutes). Add Alcohol, Stir thoroughly (1-2 minutes). Pour mixture into your chosen Jello shot containers. Refrigerate for 4 hours or until firm. Makes 8-10 2oz Jello shots.

Rain Man

3 oz pkg Orange Jello
1 cup boiling water
¼ cup cold water
½ cup 151 RUM
¼ cup MELON LIQUEUR

Mix Gelatin with hot water until dissolved (approx 2 minutes). Add cold water, stir. Let sit until steam dissipates (no more than three minutes). Add Alcohol, Stir thoroughly (1-2 minutes). Pour mixture into your chosen Jello shot containers. Refrigerate for 4 hours or until firm. Makes 8-10 2oz Jello shot.

RUM

Pain Killer

3 oz pkg Pineapple Jello
¾ cup boiling water
¼ cup cold water
1/3 cup DARK RUM
1/3 cup COCONUT RUM
1/3 cup ORANGE LIQUEUR

Mix Gelatin with hot water until dissolved (approx 2 minutes). Add cold water, stir. Let sit until steam dissipates (no more than three minutes). Add Alcohol, Stir thoroughly (1-2 minutes). Pour mixture into your chosen Jello shot containers. Refrigerate for 4 hours or until firm. Makes 8-10 2oz Jello shots.

Red Headed Step Child

3 oz pkg Cherry Jello
1 cup boiling water
½ cup cold water
½ cup SPICED RUM

Mix Gelatin with hot water until dissolved (approx 2 minutes). Add cold water, stir. Let sit until steam dissipates (no more than three minutes). Add Alcohol, Stir thoroughly (1-2 minutes). Pour mixture into your chosen Jello shot containers. Refrigerate for 4 hours or until firm. Makes 8-10 2oz Jello shots.

Fruit Stick

3 oz pkg Raspberry Jello
1 cup boiling water
½ cup cold water
½ cup BANANA RUM

Mix Gelatin with hot water until dissolved (approx 2 minutes). Add cold water, stir. Let sit until steam dissipates (no more than three minutes). Add Alcohol, Stir thoroughly (1-2 minutes). Pour mixture into your chosen Jello shot containers. Refrigerate for 4 hours or until firm. Makes 8-10 2oz Jello shots.

RUM

First Time

3 oz pkg Peach Jello
1 cup boiling water
½ cup cold water
½ cup MANGO FLAVORED RUM

Mix Gelatin with hot water until dissolved (approx 2 minutes). Add cold water, stir. Let sit until steam dissipates (no more than three minutes). Add Alcohol, Stir thoroughly (1-2 minutes). Pour mixture into your chosen Jello shot containers. Refrigerate for 4 hours or until firm. Makes 8-10 2oz Jello shots.

Peck on the Cheek

3 oz pkg Cherry Jello
3 oz pkg Orange Jello
2 cups boiling water
1 cup cold water
1 cup RUM

Mix Gelatin with hot water until dissolved (approx 2 minutes). Add cold water, stir. Let sit until steam dissipates (no more than three minutes). Add Alcohol, Stir thoroughly (1-2 minutes). Pour mixture into your chosen Jello shot containers. Refrigerate for 4 hours or until firm. Makes 16-20 2oz Jello shots.

Cloud 9

3 oz pkg Berry Blue Jello
1 cup boiling water
½ cup cold water
½ cup COCONUT RUM

Mix Gelatin with hot water until dissolved (approx 2 minutes). Add cold water, stir. Let sit until steam dissipates (no more than three minutes). Add Alcohol, Stir thoroughly (1-2 minutes). Pour mixture into your chosen Jello shot containers. Refrigerate for 4 hours or until firm. Makes 8-10 2oz Jello shots.

RUM

Pancho Villa

3 oz pkg Pineapple Jello
¾ cup boiling water
¼ cup cold water
¼ cup RUM
¼ cup GIN
¼ cup APRICOT BRANDY
¼ cup CHERRY BRANDY

Mix Gelatin with hot water until dissolved (approx 2 minutes). Add cold water, stir. Let sit until steam dissipates (no more than three minutes). Add Alcohol, Stir thoroughly (1-2 minutes). Pour mixture into your chosen Jello shot containers. Refrigerate for 4 hours or until firm. Makes 8-10 2oz Jello shots.

Tropical Sunshine

3 oz pkg Pineapple Jello
1 cup boiling water
½ cup cold water
½ cup PINEAPPLE RUM

Mix Gelatin with hot water until dissolved (approx 2 minutes). Add cold water, stir. Let sit until steam dissipates (no more than three minutes). Add Alcohol, Stir thoroughly (1-2 minutes). Pour mixture into your chosen Jello shot containers. Refrigerate for 4 hours or until firm. Makes 8-10 2oz Jello shots.

Parrot Head

3 oz pkg Pineapple Jello
1 cup boiling water
½ cup cold water
¼ cup SPICED RUM
¼ cup BLACK RASPBERRY LIQUEUR

Mix Gelatin with hot water until dissolved (approx 2 minutes). Add cold water, stir. Let sit until steam dissipates (no more than three minutes). Add Alcohol, Stir thoroughly (1-2 minutes). Pour mixture into your chosen Jello shot containers. Refrigerate for 4 hours or until firm. Makes 8-10 2oz Jello shots.

RUM

Summer Dream

3 oz pkg Strawberry Jello
1 cup boiling water
½ cup cold water
½ cup MELON RUM

Mix Gelatin with hot water until dissolved (approx 2 minutes). Add cold water, stir. Let sit until steam dissipates (no more than three minutes). Add Alcohol, Stir thoroughly (1-2 minutes). Pour mixture into your chosen Jello shot containers. Refrigerate for 4 hours or until firm. Makes 8-10 2oz Jello shots.

Killer Koolaide

6 oz pkg Cranberry Jello (or two 3 oz packages)
1 ½ cups boiling water
¾ cup cold water
½ cup VODKA
½ cup GIN
¼ cup RUM
¼ cup CHAMBORG
¼ cup TRIPLE SEC

Mix Gelatin with hot water until dissolved (approx 2 minutes). Add cold water, stir. Let sit until steam dissipates (no more than three minutes). Add Alcohol, Stir thoroughly (1-2 minutes). Pour mixture into your chosen Jello shot containers. Refrigerate for 4 hours or until firm. Makes 16-20 2oz Jello shots.

Bahama Mama

3 oz pkg Orange Jello
3 oz pkg Strawberry Jello
3 oz Pineapple Jello
3 cups boiling water
1 ½ cups cold water
1 ½ cups COCONUT RUM

Mix Gelatin with hot water until dissolved (approx 2 minutes). Add cold water, stir. Let sit until steam dissipates (no more than three minutes). Add Alcohol, Stir thoroughly (1-2 minutes). Pour mixture into your chosen Jello shot containers. Refrigerate for 4 hours or until firm. Makes 24-30 2oz Jello shots.

RUM

Beach Bum

3 oz pkg Pineapple Jello
1 cup boiling water
½ cup cold water
½ cup MANGO RUM

Mix Gelatin with hot water until dissolved (approx 2 minutes). Add cold water, stir. Let sit until steam dissipates (no more than three minutes). Add Alcohol, Stir thoroughly (1-2 minutes). Pour mixture into your chosen Jello shot containers. Refrigerate for 4 hours or until firm. Makes 8-10 2oz Jello shots.

Pirates Bounty

3 oz pkg Grape Jello
3 oz pkg Pineapple Jello
3 oz Lime Jello
2 cups boiling water
1 cup cold water
1 ½ cup COCONUT RUM
1 ½ cup VODKA

Mix Gelatin with hot water until dissolved (approx 2 minutes). Add cold water, stir. Let sit until steam dissipates (no more than three minutes). Add Alcohol, Stir thoroughly (1-2 minutes). Pour mixture into your chosen Jello shot containers. Refrigerate for 4 hours or until firm. Makes 24-30 2oz Jello shots.

Ocean Breeze

3 oz pkg Cranberry Jello
3 oz pkg Pineapple Jello
2 cups boiling water
1cup cold water
1cup COCONUT RUM

Mix Gelatin with hot water until dissolved (approx 2 minutes). Add cold water, stir. Let sit until steam dissipates (no more than three minutes). Add Alcohol, Stir thoroughly (1-2 minutes). Pour mixture into your chosen Jello shot containers. Refrigerate for 4 hours or until firm. Makes 16-20 2oz Jello shots.

RUM

Hairy Bitch

3 oz pkg Pineapple Jello
1 cup boiling water
½ cup cold water
¼ cup RUM
¼ cup TRIPLE SEC

Mix Gelatin with hot water until dissolved (approx 2 minutes). Add cold water, stir. Let sit until steam dissipates (no more than three minutes). Add Alcohol, Stir thoroughly (1-2 minutes). Pour mixture into your chosen Jello shot containers. Refrigerate for 4 hours or until firm. Makes 8-10 2oz Jello shots.

Little Devil

3 oz pkg Lemon Jello
¾ cup boiling water
¼ cup cold water
1/3 cup GIN
1/3 cup RUM
1/3 cup TRIPLE SEC

Mix Gelatin with hot water until dissolved (approx 2 minutes). Add cold water, stir. Let sit until steam dissipates (no more than three minutes). Add Alcohol, Stir thoroughly (1-2 minutes). Pour mixture into your chosen Jello shot containers. Refrigerate for 4 hours or until firm. Makes 8-10 2oz Jello shots.

Last Dance

3 oz pkg Lime Jello
1 cup boiling water
½ cup cold water
½ cup COCONUT RUM

Mix Gelatin with hot water until dissolved (approx 2 minutes). Add cold water, stir. Let sit until steam dissipates (no more than three minutes). Add Alcohol, Stir thoroughly (1-2 minutes). Pour mixture into your chosen Jello shot containers. Refrigerate for 4 hours or until firm. Makes 8-10 2oz Jello shots.

RUM

Long Kiss Goodnight!

3 oz pkg Strawberry/banana Jello
¾ cup boiling water
¼ cup cold water
1 cup COCONUT RUM

Mix Gelatin with hot water until dissolved (approx 2 minutes). Add cold water, stir. Let sit until steam dissipates (no more than three minutes). Add Alcohol, Stir thoroughly (1-2 minutes). Pour mixture into your chosen Jello shot containers. Refrigerate for 4 hours or until firm. Makes 8-10 2oz Jello shots.

Pina Colada

3 oz pkg Pineapple Jello
1 cup boiling water
¼ cup cold water
1 heaping tablespoon coconut milk concentrate (add to hot water)
¾ cup COCONUT RUM

Mix Gelatin with hot water until dissolved (approx 2 minutes). Add cold water, stir. Let sit until steam dissipates (no more than three minutes). Add Alcohol, Stir thoroughly (1-2 minutes). Pour mixture into your chosen Jello shot containers. Refrigerate for 4 hours or until firm. Makes 8-10 2oz Jello shots.

Pina Colada 2

3 oz pkg Pina Colada Jello (seasonal)
¾ cup boiling water
¼ cup cold water
½ cup COCONUT RUM
½ cup 151 RUM

Mix Gelatin with hot water until dissolved (approx 2 minutes). Add cold water, stir. Let sit until steam dissipates (no more than three minutes). Add Alcohol, Stir thoroughly (1-2 minutes). Pour mixture into your chosen Jello shot containers. Refrigerate for 4 hours or until firm. Makes 8-10 2oz Jello shots.

RUM

Panty Dropper

6 oz pkg Cherry Jello (or two 3 oz packages)
1 cup boiling water
½ cup cold water
½ cup cola
½ cup VODKA
½ cup SOUTHERN COMFORT
1/3 cup DARK RUM
1/3 cup AMARETTO
1/3 cup TEQUILA

Mix Gelatin with hot water until dissolved (approx 2 minutes). Add cold water and cola, stir. Let sit until steam dissipates (no more than three minutes). Add Alcohol, Stir thoroughly (1-2 minutes). Pour mixture into your chosen Jello shot containers. Refrigerate for 4 hours or until firm. Makes 16-20 2oz Jello shots.

SGR (Slow Gentle Ride)

3 oz pkg Mixed Fruit Jello
1 cup boiling water
½ cold water
¼ cup COCONUT RUM
¼ cup VODKA

Mix Gelatin with hot water until dissolved (approx 2 minutes). Add cold water, stir. Let sit until steam dissipates (no more than three minutes). Add Alcohol, Stir thoroughly (1-2 minutes). Pour mixture into your chosen Jello shot containers. Refrigerate for 4 hours or until firm. Makes 8-10 2oz Jello shots.

Coco-Cran

3 oz pkg Cranberry Jello
1 cup boiling water
½ cup cold water
½ cup COCONUT RUM

Mix Gelatin with hot water until dissolved (approx 2 minutes). Add cold water, stir. Let sit until steam dissipates (no more than three minutes). Add Alcohol, Stir thoroughly (1-2 minutes). Pour mixture into your chosen Jello shot containers. Refrigerate for 4 hours or until firm. Makes 8-10 2oz Jello shots.

RUM

Velvet handcuffs

3 oz Watermelon Jello
1 cup boiling water
½ cup cold water
½ cup COCONUT RUM

Mix Gelatin with hot water until dissolved (approx 2 minutes). Add cold water, stir. Let sit until steam dissipates (no more than three minutes). Add Alcohol, Stir thoroughly (1-2 minutes). Pour mixture into your chosen Jello shot containers. Refrigerate for 4 hours or until firm. Makes 8-10 2oz Jello shot

Pez

3 oz pkg Lemon Jello
1 cup boiling water
½ cup cold water
¼ cup SPICED RUM
¼ cup BLACK RASPBERRY LIQUEUR

Mix Gelatin with hot water until dissolved (approx 2 minutes). Add cold water, stir. Let sit until steam dissipates (no more than three minutes). Add Alcohol, Stir thoroughly (1-2 minutes). Pour mixture into your chosen Jello shot containers. Refrigerate for 4 hours or until firm. Makes 8-10 2oz Jello shots.

The Perfect Storm

3 oz pkg Orange Jello
3 oz pkg Pineapple Jello
2 cups boiling water
1 cup cold water
1/3 cup LIGHT RUM
1/3 cup COCONUT RUM
1/3 cup SPICED RUM

Mix Gelatin with hot water until dissolved (approx 2 minutes). Add cold water, stir. Let sit until steam dissipates (no more than three minutes). Add Alcohol, Stir thoroughly (1-2 minutes). Pour mixture into your chosen Jello shot containers. Refrigerate for 4 hours or until firm. Makes 16-20 2oz Jello shots.

RUM

Caribbean Romance

3oz pkg Orange Jello
1 cup boiling water
¼ cup cold water
¼ cup Grenadine
¼ cup AMARETTO
¼ cup PINEAPPLE RUM

Mix Gelatin with hot water until dissolved (approx 2 minutes). Add cold water, stir. Let sit until steam dissipates (no more than three minutes). Add Grenadine and Alcohol, Stir thoroughly (1-2 minutes). Pour mixture into your chosen Jello shot containers. Refrigerate for 4 hours or until firm. Makes 8-10 2oz Jello shots.

Schnapps

Schnapps

Rocky Mountain Cooler

3 oz pkg Pineapple Jello
1 cup Sprite or 7-up (heated to steaming)
¼ cup cold water
¾ cup PEACH SCHNAPPS

Mix Gelatin with hot soda until dissolved (approx 2 minutes). Add cold water, stir. Let sit until steam dissipates (no more than three minutes). Add Alcohol, Stir thoroughly (1-2 minutes). Pour mixture into your chosen Jello shot containers. Refrigerate for 4 hours or until firm. Makes 8-10 2oz Jello shots.

Pineapple Upside Down Cake

3 oz pkg pineapple Jello
¾ cup boiling water
¼ cup cold water
½ cup VODKA
¼ cup IRISH CRÈME
¼ cup BUTTERSCOTCH SCHNAPPS

Mix Gelatin with hot water until dissolved (approx 2 minutes). Add cold water, stir. Let sit until steam dissipates (no more than three minutes). Add Alcohol, Stir thoroughly (1-2 minutes). Pour mixture into your chosen Jello shot containers. Refrigerate for 4 hours or until firm. Makes 8-10 2oz Jello shots.

Bermuda Triangle

3 oz pkg Orange Jello
1 cup boiling water
½ cup cold water
¼ cup SPICED RUM
¼ cup PEACH SCHNAPPS

Mix Gelatin with hot water until dissolved (approx 2 minutes). Add cold water, stir. Let sit until steam dissipates (no more than three minutes). Add Alcohol, Stir thoroughly (1-2 minutes). Pour mixture into your chosen Jello shot containers. Refrigerate for 4 hours or until firm. Makes 8-10 2oz Jello shots.

<u>Schnapps</u>

French Tickler

3 oz pkg Orange Jello
1 cup boiling water
½ cup cold water
¼ cup CINNEMON SCHNAPPS (100 PROOF)
¼ cup VODKA

Mix Gelatin with hot water until dissolved (approx 2 minutes). Add cold water, stir. Let sit until steam dissipates (no more than three minutes). Add Alcohol, Stir thoroughly (1-2 minutes). Pour mixture into your chosen Jello shot containers. Refrigerate for 4 hours or until firm. Makes 8-10 2oz Jello shots.

Crazy Red Head

3 oz pkg Cranberry Jello
1 cup boiling water
½ cup cold water
¼ cup JAGERMEISTER
¼ cup PEACH SCHNAPPS

Mix Gelatin with hot water until dissolved (approx 2 minutes). Add cold water, stir. Let sit until steam dissipates (no more than three minutes). Add Alcohol, Stir thoroughly (1-2 minutes). Pour mixture into your chosen Jello shot containers. Refrigerate for 4 hours or until firm. Makes 8-10 2oz Jello shots.

Bitch Fight

3oz pkg Cranberry Jello
1 cup boiling water
¼ cup cold water
¼ cup Lime Juice
¼ cup PEACH SCHNAPPS
¼ cup ORANGE LIQUEUR

Mix Gelatin with hot water until dissolved (approx 2 minutes). Add cold water, and lime juice. Stir. Let sit until steam dissipates (no more than three minutes). Add Alcohol, Stir thoroughly (1-2 minutes). Pour mixture into your chosen Jello shot containers. Refrigerate for 4 hours or until firm. Makes 8-10 2oz Jello shots.

Schnapps

The Girl Next Door

3 oz pkg Cranberry Jello
1 cup boiling water
½ cup cold water
½ cup PEACH SCHNAPPS

Mix Gelatin with hot water until dissolved (approx 2 minutes). Add cold water, stir. Let sit until steam dissipates (no more than three minutes). Add Alcohol, Stir thoroughly (1-2 minutes). Pour mixture into your chosen Jello shot containers. Refrigerate for 4 hours or until firm. Makes 8-10 2oz Jello shots.

Comfortable Fuzzy Screw Against the Wall

3 oz pkg Orange Jello
¾ cup boiling water
¼ cup cold water
1/3 cup SOUTHERN COMFORT
1/3 cup PEACH SCHNAPPS
1/3 cup VODKA

Mix Gelatin with hot water until dissolved (approx 2 minutes). Add cold water, stir. Let sit until steam dissipates (no more than three minutes). Add Alcohol, Stir thoroughly (1-2 minutes). Pour mixture into your chosen Jello shot containers. Refrigerate for 4 hours or until firm. Makes 8-10 2oz Jello shots.

Twin Peach

3 oz pkg Peach Jello
1 cup boiling water
½ cup cold water
½ cup PEACH SCHNAPPS

Mix Gelatin with hot water until dissolved (approx 2 minutes). Add cold water, stir. Let sit until steam dissipates (no more than three minutes). Add Alcohol, Stir thoroughly (1-2 minutes). Pour mixture into your chosen Jello shot containers. Refrigerate for 4 hours or until firm. Makes 8-10 2oz Jello shots.

Schnapps

Juicy Fruit

3 oz pkg Pineapple Jello
¾ cup boiling water
¼ cup cold water
1/3 cup VODKA
1/3 cup PEACH SCHNAPPS
1/3 cup MELON LIQUEUR

Mix Gelatin with hot water until dissolved (approx 2 minutes). Add cold water, stir. Let sit until steam dissipates (no more than three minutes). Add Alcohol, Stir thoroughly (1-2 minutes). Pour mixture into your chosen Jello shot containers. Refrigerate for 4 hours or until firm. Makes 8-10 2oz Jello shots.

Leprechaun

3 oz orange Jello
¾ cup boiling water
¼ cup cold water
1/3 cup PEACH SCHNAPPS
1/3 cup PEACH VODKA
1/3 cup BLUE CURACOA

Mix Gelatin with hot water until dissolved (approx 2 minutes). Add cold water, stir. Let sit until steam dissipates (no more than three minutes). Add Alcohol, Stir thoroughly (1-2 minutes). Pour mixture into your chosen Jello shot containers. Refrigerate for 4 hours or until firm. Makes 8-10 2oz Jello shots.

Georgia Peach

3 oz pkg Mixed Fruit Jello
1 cup boiling water
½ cup cold water
½ cup PEACH SCHNAPPS

Mix Gelatin with hot water until dissolved (approx 2 minutes). Add cold water, stir. Let sit until steam dissipates (no more than three minutes). Add Alcohol, Stir thoroughly (1-2 minutes). Pour mixture into your chosen Jello shot containers. Refrigerate for 4 hours or until firm. Makes 8-10 2oz Jello shots.

Schnapps

Melon Cooler

6 oz pkg Pineapple Jello (or two 3 oz packages)
2 cups boiling water
1 cup cold water
½ cup MELON LIQUEUR
¼ cup PEACH SCHNAPPS
¼ cup RASPBERRY SCHNAPPS

Mix Gelatin with hot water until dissolved (approx 2 minutes). Add cold water, stir. Let sit until steam dissipates (no more than three minutes). Add Alcohol, Stir thoroughly (1-2 minutes). Pour mixture into your chosen Jello shot containers. Refrigerate for 4 hours or until firm. Makes 16-20 2oz Jello shots.

June Bug

3 oz pkg Pineapple Jello
3 oz pkg Cranberry Jello
2 cups boiling water
1 cup cold water
1/3 cup BANANA LIQUEUR
1/3 cup MELON LIQUEUR
1/3 cup PEACH SCHNAPPS

Mix Gelatin with hot water until dissolved (approx 2 minutes). Add cold water, stir. Let sit until steam dissipates (no more than three minutes). Add Alcohol, Stir thoroughly (1-2 minutes). Pour mixture into your chosen Jello shot containers. Refrigerate for 4 hours or until firm. Makes 16-20 2oz Jello shots.

Sex on the Beach

3 oz pkg Cranberry Jello
3 oz pkg Orange Jello
2 cups boiling water
½ cup cold water
¾ cup PEACH SCHNAPPS
¾ cup VODKA

Mix Gelatin with hot water until dissolved (approx 2 minutes). Add cold water, stir. Let sit until steam dissipates (no more than three minutes). Add Alcohol, Stir thoroughly (1-2 minutes). Pour mixture into your chosen Jello shot containers. Refrigerate for 4 hours or until firm. Makes 16-20 2oz Jello shots.

Schnapps

Fuzzy Navel

3 oz pkg Lime Jello
3 oz pkg Lemon Jello
2 cups boiling water
½ cup cold water
¾ cup PEACH SCHNAPPS
¾ cup VODKA

Mix Gelatin with hot water until dissolved (approx 2 minutes). Add cold water, stir. Let sit until steam dissipates (no more than three minutes). Add Alcohol, Stir thoroughly (1-2 minutes). Pour mixture into your chosen Jello shot containers. Refrigerate for 4 hours or until firm. Makes 16-20 2oz Jello shots.

Bottle Caps

3 oz pkg Lime Jello
¾ cup boiling water
¼ cup cold water
½ cup ROOTBEER SCHNAPPS
½ cup RASPBERRY VODKA

Mix Gelatin with hot water until dissolved (approx 2 minutes). Add cold water, stir. Let sit until steam dissipates (no more than three minutes). Add Alcohol, Stir thoroughly (1-2 minutes). Pour mixture into your chosen Jello shot containers. Refrigerate for 4 hours or until firm. Makes 8-10 2oz Jello shots.

Strawberry Margarita

6 oz pkg Margarita Jello (or two 3 oz packages)
1 ½ cups boiling water
½ cup cold water
1 cup STRAWBERRY SCHNAPPS
¾ cup TEQUILA
¼ cup TRIPLE SEC

Mix Gelatin with hot water until dissolved (approx 2 minutes). Add cold water, stir. Let sit until steam dissipates (no more than three minutes). Add Alcohol, Stir thoroughly (1-2 minutes). Pour mixture into your chosen Jello shot containers. Refrigerate for 4 hours or until firm. Makes 16-20 2oz Jello shots.

Schnapps

Strawberry Sunrise

3 oz pkg Orange Jello
1 cup boiling water
¼ cup cold water
¼ cup Grenadine
½ cup STRAWBERRY SCHNAPPS

Mix Gelatin with hot water until dissolved (approx 2 minutes). Add cold water, stir. Let sit until steam dissipates (no more than three minutes). Add Alcohol and Grenadine, Stir thoroughly (1-2 minutes). Pour mixture into your chosen Jello shot containers. Refrigerate for 4 hours or until firm. Makes 8-10 2oz Jello shots.

Backseat Betty

3 oz pkg Cranberry Jello
1 cup boiling water
½ cup cold water
½ cup PEACH SCHNAPPS

Mix Gelatin with hot water until dissolved (approx 2 minutes). Add cold water, stir. Let sit until steam dissipates (no more than three minutes). Add Alcohol, Stir thoroughly (1-2 minutes). Pour mixture into your chosen Jello shot containers. Refrigerate for 4 hours or until firm. Makes 8-10 2oz Jello shots.

Burning Sun

3 oz pkg Pineapple Jello
1 cup boiling water
½ cup cold water
½ cup STRAWBERRY SCHNAPPS

Mix Gelatin with hot water until dissolved (approx 2 minutes). Add cold water, stir. Let sit until steam dissipates (no more than three minutes). Add Alcohol, Stir thoroughly (1-2 minutes). Pour mixture into your chosen Jello shot containers. Refrigerate for 4 hours or until firm. Makes 8-10 2oz Jello shots.

Schnapps

Sex with a Straw

3 oz pkg Strawberry Jello
1 cup boiling water
½ cup cold water
¼ cup STRAWBERRY SCHNAPPS
¼ cup VODKA

Mix Gelatin with hot water until dissolved (approx 2 minutes). Add cold water, stir. Let sit until steam dissipates (no more than three minutes). Add Alcohol, Stir thoroughly (1-2 minutes). Pour mixture into your chosen Jello shot containers. Refrigerate for 4 hours or until firm. Makes 8-10 2oz Jello shots.

Red Silk Panties

3 oz pkg Cranberry Jello
1 cup boiling water
½ cup cold water
¼ cup VODKA
¼ cup PEACH SCHNAPPS

Mix Gelatin with hot water until dissolved (approx 2 minutes). Add cold water, stir. Let sit until steam dissipates (no more than three minutes). Add Alcohol, Stir thoroughly (1-2 minutes). Pour mixture into your chosen Jello shot containers. Refrigerate for 4 hours or until firm. Makes 8-10 2oz Jello shots.

Tijuana Taxi

6 oz pkg Lemon Jello (or two 3 oz packages)
2 cups boiling water
1 cup cold water
½ cup TEQUILA
¼ cup BLUE CURACOU
¼ cup TROPICAL FRUIT SCHNAPPS

Mix Gelatin with hot water until dissolved (approx 2 minutes). Add cold water, stir. Let sit until steam dissipates (no more than three minutes). Add Alcohol, Stir thoroughly (1-2 minutes). Pour mixture into your chosen Jello shot containers. Refrigerate for 4 hours or until firm. Makes 16-20 2oz Jello shots.

Schnapps

Pink Snapper

3 oz pkg Cranberry Jello
1 cup boiling water
½ cup cold water
¼ cup PEACH SCHNAPPS
¼ cup KENTUCKY WHISKEY

Mix Gelatin with hot water until dissolved (approx 2 minutes). Add cold water, stir. Let sit until steam dissipates (no more than three minutes). Add Alcohol, Stir thoroughly (1-2 minutes). Pour mixture into your chosen Jello shot containers. Refrigerate for 4 hours or until firm. Makes 8-10 2oz Jello shots.

Jungle Juice

3 oz pkg Mixed Fruit Jello
¾ cup boiling water
¼ cup cold water
¼ cup EVERCLEAR
¾ cup WILDBERRY SCHNAPPS

Mix Gelatin with hot water until dissolved (approx 2 minutes). Add cold water, stir. Let sit until steam dissipates (no more than three minutes). Add Alcohol, Stir thoroughly (1-2 minutes). Pour mixture into your chosen Jello shot containers. Refrigerate for 4 hours or until firm. Makes 8-10 2oz Jello shots.

Tequila

Tequila

Broken Sombrero

3 oz Lime Jello
1 cup boiling water
½ cup cold water
½ cup TEQUILA

Mix Gelatin with hot water until dissolved (approx 2 minutes). Add cold water, stir. Let sit until steam dissipates (no more than three minutes). Add Alcohol, Stir thoroughly (1-2 minutes). Pour mixture into your chosen Jello shot containers. Refrigerate for 4 hours or until firm. Makes 8-10 2oz Jello shots.

Tequila Sunrise

3 oz pkg Orange Jello
¾ cup boiling water
½ cup cold water
¼ cup Grenadine
½ cup TEQUILA

Mix Gelatin with hot water until dissolved (approx 2 minutes). Add cold water, stir. Let sit until steam dissipates (no more than three minutes). Add Alcohol and Grenadine, Stir thoroughly (1-2 minutes). Pour mixture into your chosen Jello shot containers. Refrigerate for 4 hours or until firm. Makes 8-10 2oz Jello shots.

Margarita

3 oz pkg Margarita Jello (seasonal)
1 cup heated Margarita Mix
1 tsp Lime Juice
¼ cup cold water
¾ cup TEQUILA

Mix Gelatin with hot Margarita mix until dissolved (approx 2 minutes). Add cold water, stir. Let sit until steam dissipates (no more than three minutes). Add Alcohol, Stir thoroughly (1-2 minutes). Pour mixture into your chosen Jello shot containers. Refrigerate for 4 hours or until firm. Sprinkle with salt prior to serving. Makes 8-10 2oz Jello shots.

Tequila

Panty Dropper

6 oz pkg Cherry Jello (or two 3 oz packages)
1 cup boiling water
½ cup cold water
½ cup cola
½ cup VODKA
½ cup SOUTHERN COMFORT
1/3 cup DARK RUM
1/3 cup AMARETTO
1/3 cup TEQUILA

Mix Gelatin with hot water until dissolved (approx 2 minutes). Add cold water and cola, stir. Let sit until steam dissipates (no more than three minutes). Add Alcohol, Stir thoroughly (1-2 minutes). Pour mixture into your chosen Jello shot containers. Refrigerate for 4 hours or until firm. Makes 16-20 2oz Jello shots.

Gentle Ben

3 oz pkg Orange Jello
¾ cup boiling water
½ cup cold water
¼ cup GIN
¼ cup TEQUILA
¼ cup VODKA

Mix Gelatin with hot water until dissolved (approx 2 minutes). Add cold water, stir. Let sit until steam dissipates (no more than three minutes). Add Alcohol, Stir thoroughly (1-2 minutes). Pour mixture into your chosen Jello shot containers. Refrigerate for 4 hours or until firm. Makes 8-10 2oz Jello shots.

Tijuana Taxi

6 oz pkg Lemon Jello (or two 3 oz packages)
2 cups boiling water
1 cup cold water
½ cup TEQUILA
¼ cup BLUE CURACOU
¼ cup TROPICAL FRUIT SCHNAPPS

Mix Gelatin with hot water until dissolved (approx 2 minutes). Add cold water, stir. Let sit until steam dissipates (no more than three minutes). Add Alcohol, Stir thoroughly (1-2 minutes). Pour mixture into your chosen Jello shot containers. Refrigerate for 4 hours or until firm. Makes 16-20 2oz Jello shots.

Tequila

Strawberry Margarita

3 oz pkg of Margarita Jello (seasonal)
1 cup boiling water
½ cup cold water
½ cup TEQUILA ROSE

Mix Gelatin with hot water until dissolved (approx 2 minutes). Add cold water, stir. Let sit until steam dissipates (no more than three minutes). Add Alcohol, Stir thoroughly (1-2 minutes). Pour mixture into your chosen Jello shot containers. Refrigerate for 4 hours or until firm. Makes 8-10 2oz Jello shots.

Long Island Iced Tea

6 oz pkg Lemon Jello (or two 3 oz packages)
1 cup boiling water
½ cup cola
½ cup cold water
½ cup GIN
½ cup LIGHT RUM
½ cup VODKA
½ cup TEQUILA

Mix Gelatin with hot water until dissolved (approx 2 minutes). Add cold water and cola, stir. Let sit until steam dissipates (no more than three minutes). Add Alcohol, Stir thoroughly (1-2 minutes). Pour mixture into your chosen Jello shot containers. Refrigerate for 4 hours or until firm. Makes 16-20 2oz Jello shots.

Nuclear Meltdown

6 oz pkg Pineapple Jello (or two 3 oz packages)
1 1/2 cups boiling water
½ cup cold water
¼ cup GIN
¼ cup TRIPLE SEC
½ cup VODKA
½ cup RUM
½ cup TEQUILA

Mix Gelatin with hot water until dissolved (approx 2 minutes). Add cold water, stir. Let sit until steam dissipates (no more than three minutes). Add Alcohol, Stir thoroughly (1-2 minutes). Pour mixture into your chosen Jello shot containers. Refrigerate for 4 hours or until firm. Makes 16-20 2oz Jello shots.

Tequila

Piñata

3 oz pkg Lime Jello
1 cup boiling water
½ cup cold water
¼ cup TEQUILA
¼ cup BANANA LIQUEUR

Mix Gelatin with hot water until dissolved (approx 2 minutes). Add cold water, stir. Let sit until steam dissipates (no more than three minutes). Add Alcohol, Stir thoroughly (1-2 minutes). Pour mixture into your chosen Jello shot containers. Refrigerate for 4 hours or until firm. Makes 8-10 2oz Jello shots.

Mockingbird

3 oz pkg Lime Jello
1 cup boiling water
½ cup cold water
¼ cup TEQUILA
¼ cup CRÈME DE MENTHE (white)

Mix Gelatin with hot water until dissolved (approx 2 minutes). Add cold water, stir. Let sit until steam dissipates (no more than three minutes). Add Alcohol, Stir thoroughly (1-2 minutes). Pour mixture into your chosen Jello shot containers. Refrigerate for 4 hours or until firm. Makes 8-10 2oz Jello shots.

Moon Racker

3 oz pkg Pineapple Jello
1 cup boiling water
½ cup cold water
¼ cup TEQUILA
¼ cup BLUE CURACOA

Mix Gelatin with hot water until dissolved (approx 2 minutes). Add cold water, stir. Let sit until steam dissipates (no more than three minutes). Add Alcohol, Stir thoroughly (1-2 minutes). Pour mixture into your chosen Jello shot containers. Refrigerate for 4 hours or until firm. Makes 8-10 2oz Jello shots.

Tequila

Mexican Screw

3 oz pkg Orange Jello
1 cup boiling water
½ cup cold water
½ cup TEQUILA

Mix Gelatin with hot water until dissolved (approx 2 minutes). Add cold water, stir. Let sit until steam dissipates (no more than three minutes). Add Alcohol, Stir thoroughly (1-2 minutes). Pour mixture into your chosen Jello shot containers. Refrigerate for 4 hours or until firm. Makes 8-10 2oz Jello shots.

Triple Sec

Triple Sec

Hawaiian Sunrise

3 oz pkg Pineapple Jello
1 cup boiling water
½ cup cold water
¼ cup GIN
¼ cup TRIPLE SEC

Mix Gelatin with hot water until dissolved (approx 2 minutes). Add cold water, stir. Let sit until steam dissipates (no more than three minutes). Add Alcohol, Stir thoroughly (1-2 minutes). Pour mixture into your chosen Jello shot containers. Refrigerate for 4 hours or until firm. Makes 8-10 2oz Jello shots.

Alfie Cocktail

3 oz Pineapple Jello
¾ cup boiling water
¼ cup cold water
¾ cup LEMON VODKA
¼ cup TRIPLE SEC

Mix Gelatin with hot water until dissolved (approx 2 minutes). Add cold water, stir. Let sit until steam dissipates (no more than three minutes). Add Alcohol, Stir thoroughly (1-2 minutes). Pour mixture into your chosen Jello shot containers. Refrigerate for 4 hours or until firm. Makes 8-10 2oz Jello shots.

Killer Whale

3 oz pkg Cranberry Jello
3 oz pkg Orange Jello
2 cups boiling water
1 cup cold water
¼ cup VODKA
¼ cup RUM
¼ cup BLACK RASPBERRY LIQUEUR
¼ cup TRIPLE SEC

Mix Gelatin with hot water until dissolved (approx 2 minutes). Add cold water, stir. Let sit until steam dissipates (no more than three minutes). Add Alcohol, Stir thoroughly (1-2 minutes). Pour mixture into your chosen Jello shot containers. Refrigerate for 4 hours or until firm. Makes 16-20 2oz Jello shots.

Triple Sec

Major Tom

3 oz pkg Orange Jello
¾ cup boiling water
¼ cup cold water
1/3 cup CHERRY VODKA
1/3 cup TRIPLE SEC
1/3 cup CHERRY BRANDY

Mix Gelatin with hot water until dissolved (approx 2 minutes). Add cold water, stir. Let sit until steam dissipates (no more than three minutes). Add Alcohol, Stir thoroughly (1-2 minutes). Pour mixture into your chosen Jello shot containers. Refrigerate for 4 hours or until firm. Makes 8-10 2oz Jello shots.

Sweet – n- Sour

3 oz pkg Lime Jello
¾ cup boiling water
½ cup cold water
¼ cup TRIPLE SEC
½ cup VODKA

Mix Gelatin with hot water until dissolved (approx 2 minutes). Add cold water, stir. Let sit until steam dissipates (no more than three minutes). Add Alcohol, Stir thoroughly (1-2 minutes). Pour mixture into your chosen Jello shot containers. Refrigerate for 4 hours or until firm. Makes 8-10 2oz Jello shots.

Killer Koolaide

6 oz pkg Cranberry Jello (or two 3 oz packages)
1½ cups boiling water
¾ cup cold water
½ cup VODKA
½ cup GIN
¼ cup RUM
¼ cup CHAMBORG
¼ cup TRIPLE SEC

Mix Gelatin with hot water until dissolved (approx 2 minutes). Add cold water, stir. Let sit until steam dissipates (no more than three minutes). Add Alcohol, Stir thoroughly (1-2 minutes). Pour mixture into your chosen Jello shot containers. Refrigerate for 4 hours or until firm. Makes 16-20 2oz Jello shots.

Triple Sec

Little Devil

3 oz pkg Lemon Jello
¾ cup boiling water
¼ cup cold water
1/3 cup GIN
1/3 cup RUM
1/3 cup TRIPLE SEC

Mix Gelatin with hot water until dissolved (approx 2 minutes). Add cold water, stir. Let sit until steam dissipates (no more than three minutes). Add Alcohol, Stir thoroughly (1-2 minutes). Pour mixture into your chosen Jello shot containers. Refrigerate for 4 hours or until firm. Makes 8-10 2oz Jello shots.

Nuclear Meltdown

6 oz pkg Pineapple Jello (or two 3 oz packages)
1 1/2 cups boiling water
½ cup cold water
¼ cup GIN
¼ cup TRIPLE SEC
½ cup VODKA
½ cup RUM
½ cup TEQUILA

Mix Gelatin with hot water until dissolved (approx 2 minutes). Add cold water, stir. Let sit until steam dissipates (no more than three minutes). Add Alcohol, Stir thoroughly (1-2 minutes). Pour mixture into your chosen Jello shot containers. Refrigerate for 4 hours or until firm. Makes 16-20 2oz Jello shots.

Kamikaze

3 oz pkg Lime Jello
¾ cup boiling water
½ cup cold water
½ cup VODKA
¼ cup TRIPLE SEC

Mix Gelatin with hot water until dissolved (approx 2 minutes). Add cold water, stir. Let sit until steam dissipates (no more than three minutes). Add Alcohol, Stir thoroughly (1-2 minutes). Pour mixture into your chosen Jello shot containers. Refrigerate for 4 hours or until firm. Makes 16-20 2oz Jello shots.

Triple Sec

After Dinner Shot

3 oz pkg Lime Jello
1 cup boiling water
½ cup cold water
¼ cup APRICOT FLAVORED BRANDY
¼ cup TRIPLE SEC

Mix Gelatin with hot water until dissolved (approx 2 minutes). Add cold water, stir. Let sit until steam dissipates (no more than three minutes). Add Alcohol, Stir thoroughly (1-2 minutes). Pour mixture into your chosen Jello shot containers. Refrigerate for 4 hours or until firm. Makes 8-10 2oz Jello shots.

Boston Sidecar

3 oz pkg Lime Jello
1 cup boiling water
¼ cup cold water
¼ cup BRANDY
¼ cup LIGHT RUM
¼ cup TRIPLE SEC

Mix Gelatin with hot water until dissolved (approx 2 minutes). Add cold water, stir. Let sit until steam dissipates (no more than three minutes). Add Alcohol, Stir thoroughly (1-2 minutes). Pour mixture into your chosen Jello shot containers. Refrigerate for 4 hours or until firm. Makes 8-10 2oz Jello shots.

Between the Sheets

3 oz pkg Lemon Jello
¾ cup boiling water
½ cup cold water
¼ cup BRANDY
¼ cup TRIPLE SEC
¼ cup LIGHT RUM

Mix Gelatin with hot water until dissolved (approx 2 minutes). Add cold water, stir. Let sit until steam dissipates (no more than three minutes). Add Alcohol, Stir thoroughly (1-2 minutes). Pour mixture into your chosen Jello shot containers. Refrigerate for 4 hours or until firm. Makes 8-10 2oz Jello shots.

Triple Sec

Grass Skirt

3 oz pkg Pineapple Jello
1 cup boiling water
½ cup cold water
splash of Grenadine
¼ cup GIN
¼ cup TRIPLE SEC

Mix Gelatin with hot water until dissolved (approx 2 minutes). Add cold water, splash of grenadine, and stir. Let sit until steam dissipates (no more than three minutes). Add Alcohol, Stir thoroughly (1-2 minutes). Pour mixture into your chosen Jello shot containers. Refrigerate for 4 hours or until firm. Makes 8-10 2oz Jello shots.

Hairy Bitch

3 oz pkg Pineapple Jello
1 cup boiling water
½ cup cold water
¼ cup RUM
¼ cup TRIPLE SEC

Mix Gelatin with hot water until dissolved (approx 2 minutes). Add cold water, stir. Let sit until steam dissipates (no more than three minutes). Add Alcohol, Stir thoroughly (1-2 minutes). Pour mixture into your chosen Jello shot containers. Refrigerate for 4 hours or until firm. Makes 8-10 2oz Jello shots.

Life Savor

3 oz pkg Orange Jello
¾ cup boiling water
¼ cup cold water
1/3 cup TRIPLE SEC
1/3 cup MELON LIQUEUR
1/3 cup COCONUT RUM

Mix Gelatin with hot water until dissolved (approx 2 minutes). Add cold water, stir. Let sit until steam dissipates (no more than three minutes). Add Alcohol, Stir thoroughly (1-2 minutes). Pour mixture into your chosen Jello shot containers. Refrigerate for 4 hours or until firm. Makes 8-10 2oz Jello shots.

Vodka

Vodka

Bull Frog

3 oz pkg Lemon Jello
1 cup boiling water
½ cup cold water
½ cup VODKA

Mix Gelatin with hot water until dissolved (approx 2 minutes). Add cold water, stir. Let sit until steam dissipates (no more than three minutes). Add Alcohol, Stir thoroughly (1-2 minutes). Pour mixture into your chosen Jello shot containers. Refrigerate for 4 hours or until firm. Makes 8-10 2oz Jello shots.

Vodka Cran

3 oz pkg Cranberry Jello
3 oz pkg Lime Jello
2 cup boiling water
1 cup cold water
1 cup VODKA

Mix Gelatin with hot water until dissolved (approx 2 minutes). Add cold water, stir. Let sit until steam dissipates (no more than three minutes). Add Alcohol, Stir thoroughly (1-2 minutes). Pour mixture into your chosen Jello shot containers. Refrigerate for 4 hours or until firm. Makes 16-20 2oz Jello shots.

Broken Heart

3 oz pkg Orange Jello
1 cup boiling water
½ cup cold water
¼ cup VODKA
¼ cup BLACK RASPBERRY LIQUEUR

Mix Gelatin with hot water until dissolved (approx 2 minutes). Add cold water, stir. Let sit until steam dissipates (no more than three minutes). Add Alcohol, Stir thoroughly (1-2 minutes). Pour mixture into your chosen Jello shot containers. Refrigerate for 4 hours or until firm. Makes 8-10 2oz Jello shots.

Vodka

Broken Down Golf Cart

3 oz pkg Cranberry Jello
1 cup boiling water
½ cup cold water
¼ cup VODKA
¼ cup AMARETTO

Mix Gelatin with hot water until dissolved (approx 2 minutes). Add cold water, stir. Let sit until steam dissipates (no more than three minutes). Add Alcohol, Stir thoroughly (1-2 minutes). Pour mixture into your chosen Jello shot containers. Refrigerate for 4 hours or until firm. Makes 8-10 2oz Jello shots.

French Tickler

3 oz pkg Orange Jello
1 cup boiling water
½ cup cold water
¼ cup CINNEMON SCHNAPPS (100 PROOF)
¼ cup VODKA

Mix Gelatin with hot water until dissolved (approx 2 minutes). Add cold water, stir. Let sit until steam dissipates (no more than three minutes). Add Alcohol, Stir thoroughly (1-2 minutes). Pour mixture into your chosen Jello shot containers. Refrigerate for 4 hours or until firm. Makes 8-10 2oz Jello shots.

Purple Haze

3 oz pkg Cranberry Jello
1 cup boiling water
½ cup cold water
¼ cup VODKA
¼ cup BLACK RASPBERRY LIQUEUR

Mix Gelatin with hot water until dissolved (approx 2 minutes). Add cold water, stir. Let sit until steam dissipates (no more than three minutes). Add Alcohol, Stir thoroughly (1-2 minutes). Pour mixture into your chosen Jello shot containers. Refrigerate for 4 hours or until firm. Makes 8-10 2oz Jello shots.

Vodka

Vodka Gimlet

3 oz pkg Lime Jello
1 cup boiling water
½ cup Rose's Lime Juice
½ cup VODKA

Mix Gelatin with hot water until dissolved (approx 2 minutes). Add chilled Lime Juice, stir. Let sit until steam dissipates (no more than three minutes). Add Alcohol, Stir thoroughly (1-2 minutes). Pour mixture into your chosen Jello shot containers. Refrigerate for 4 hours or until firm. Makes 8-10 2oz Jello shots.

Kamikaze

3 oz pkg Lime Jello
¾ cup boiling water
½ cup cold water
½ cup VODKA
¼ cup TRIPLE SEC

Mix Gelatin with hot water until dissolved (approx 2 minutes). Add cold water, stir. Let sit until steam dissipates (no more than three minutes). Add Alcohol, Stir thoroughly (1-2 minutes). Pour mixture into your chosen Jello shot containers. Refrigerate for 4 hours or until firm. Makes 8-10 2oz Jello shots.

Madras

3 oz pkg Orange Jello
3 oz pkg Cranberry Jello
2 cups boiling water
1 cup cold water
1 cup ORANGE VODKA

Mix Gelatin with hot water until dissolved (approx 2 minutes). Add cold water, stir. Let sit until steam dissipates (no more than three minutes). Add Alcohol, Stir thoroughly (1-2 minutes). Pour mixture into your chosen Jello shot containers. Refrigerate for 4 hours or until firm. Makes 16-20 2oz Jello shots.

Vodka

Purple Hooter

3 oz pkg Lime Jello
1 cup boiling water
½ cup cold water
¼ cup VODKA
¼ cup BLACK RASPBERRY LIQUEUR

Mix Gelatin with hot water until dissolved (approx 2 minutes). Add cold water, stir. Let sit until steam dissipates (no more than three minutes). Add Alcohol, Stir thoroughly (1-2 minutes). Pour mixture into your chosen Jello shot containers. Refrigerate for 4 hours or until firm. Makes 8-10 2oz Jello shots.

Red Silk Panties

3 oz pkg Cranberry Jello
1 cup boiling water
½ cup cold water
¼ cup VODKA
¼ cup PEACH SCHNAPPS

Mix Gelatin with hot water until dissolved (approx 2 minutes). Add cold water, stir. Let sit until steam dissipates (no more than three minutes). Add Alcohol, Stir thoroughly (1-2 minutes). Pour mixture into your chosen Jello shot containers. Refrigerate for 4 hours or until firm. Makes 8-10 2oz Jello shots.

Major Tom

3 oz pkg Orange Jello
¾ cup boiling water
¼ cup cold water
1/3 cup CHERRY VODKA
1/3 cup TRIPLE SEC
1/3 cup CHERRY BRANDY

Mix Gelatin with hot water until dissolved (approx 2 minutes). Add cold water, stir. Let sit until steam dissipates (no more than three minutes). Add Alcohol, Stir thoroughly (1-2 minutes). Pour mixture into your chosen Jello shot containers. Refrigerate for 4 hours or until firm. Makes 8-10 2oz Jello shots.

Vodka

G-spot

3 oz pkg Cranberry Jello
1 cup boiling water
½ cup cold water
¼ cup VODKA
¼ cup ORANGE LIQUEUR

Mix Gelatin with hot water until dissolved (approx 2 minutes). Add cold water, stir. Let sit until steam dissipates (no more than three minutes). Add Alcohol, Stir thoroughly (1-2 minutes). Pour mixture into your chosen Jello shot containers. Refrigerate for 4 hours or until firm. Makes 8-10 2oz Jello shots.

Bomb Pop

3 oz pkg Lemon Jello
¾ cup boiling water
½ cup cold water
½ cup RASPBERRY VODKA
¼ cup BLUE CURACOA

Mix Gelatin with hot water until dissolved (approx 2 minutes). Add cold water, stir. Let sit until steam dissipates (no more than three minutes). Add Alcohol, Stir thoroughly (1-2 minutes). Pour mixture into your chosen Jello shot containers. Refrigerate for 4 hours or until firm. Makes 8-10 2oz Jello shots.

Brass Monkey

3 oz pkg Orange Jello
1 cup boiling water
½ cup cold water
¼ cup RUM
¼ cup VODKA

Mix Gelatin with hot water until dissolved (approx 2 minutes). Add cold water, stir. Let sit until steam dissipates (no more than three minutes). Add Alcohol, Stir thoroughly (1-2 minutes). Pour mixture into your chosen Jello shot containers. Refrigerate for 4 hours or until firm. Makes 8-10 2oz Jello shots.

<u>Vodka</u>

Leprechaun

3 oz orange Jello
¾ cup boiling water
¼ cup cold water
1/3 cup PEACH SCHNAPPS
1/3 cup PEACH VODKA
1/3 cup BLUE CURACOA

Mix Gelatin with hot water until dissolved (approx 2 minutes). Add cold water, stir. Let sit until steam dissipates (no more than three minutes). Add Alcohol, Stir thoroughly (1-2 minutes). Pour mixture into your chosen Jello shot containers. Refrigerate for 4 hours or until firm. Makes 8-10 2oz Jello shots.

Panty Dropper

6 oz pkg Cherry Jello (or two 3 oz packages)
1 cup boiling water
½ cup cold water
½ cup cola
½ cup VODKA
½ cup SOUTHERN COMFORT
1/3 cup DARK RUM
1/3 cup AMARETTO
1/3 cup TEQUILA

Mix Gelatin with hot water until dissolved (approx 2 minutes). Add cold water and cola, stir. Let sit until steam dissipates (no more than three minutes). Add Alcohol, Stir thoroughly (1-2 minutes). Pour mixture into your chosen Jello shot containers. Refrigerate for 4 hours or until firm. Makes 16-20 2oz Jello shots.

Vodka

Nuclear Meltdown

6 oz pkg Pineapple Jello (or two 3 oz packages)
1 1/2 cups boiling water
½ cup cold water
¼ cup GIN
¼ cup TRIPLE SEC
½ cup VODKA
½ cup RUM
½ cup TEQUILA

Mix Gelatin with hot water until dissolved (approx 2 minutes). Add cold water, stir. Let sit until steam dissipates (no more than three minutes). Add Alcohol, Stir thoroughly (1-2 minutes). Pour mixture into your chosen Jello shot containers. Refrigerate for 4 hours or until firm. Makes 16-20 2oz Jello shots.

Banana Split

3 oz pkg Strawberry Jello
1 cup boiling water
¼ cup cold water
¼ cup VODKA
¼ cup BANANA LIQUEUR
¼ cup CRÈME DE COCAO

Mix Gelatin with hot water until dissolved (approx 2 minutes). Add cold water, stir. Let sit until steam dissipates (no more than three minutes). Add Alcohol, Stir thoroughly (1-2 minutes). Pour mixture into your chosen Jello shot containers. Refrigerate for 4 hours or until firm. Makes 8-10 2oz Jello shots.

Purple Dinosaur

3 oz pkg Grape Jello
1 cup boiling water
½ cup cold water
½ cup VODKA

Mix Gelatin with hot water until dissolved (approx 2 minutes). Add cold water, stir. Let sit until steam dissipates (no more than three minutes). Add Alcohol, Stir thoroughly (1-2 minutes). Pour mixture into your chosen Jello shot containers. Refrigerate for 4 hours or until firm. Makes 8-10 2oz Jello shots.

Vodka

Blueberry Bandaide

3 oz pkg Berry Blue Jello
1 cup boiling water
½ cup cold water
½ cup WATERMELON VODKA

Mix Gelatin with hot water until dissolved (approx 2 minutes). Add cold water, stir. Let sit until steam dissipates (no more than three minutes). Add Alcohol, Stir thoroughly (1-2 minutes). Pour mixture into your chosen Jello shot containers. Refrigerate for 4 hours or until firm. Makes 8-10 2oz Jello shots.

Killer Koolaide

6 oz pkg Cranberry Jello (or two 3 oz packages)
1 ½ cups boiling water
¾ cup cold water
½ cup VODKA
½ cup GIN
¼ cup RUM
¼ cup CHAMBORG
¼ cup TRIPLE SEC

Mix Gelatin with hot water until dissolved (approx 2 minutes). Add cold water, stir. Let sit until steam dissipates (no more than three minutes). Add Alcohol, Stir thoroughly (1-2 minutes). Pour mixture into your chosen Jello shot containers. Refrigerate for 4 hours or until firm. Makes 16-20 2oz Jello shots.

Killer Whale

3 oz pkg Cranberry Jello
3 oz pkg Orange Jello
2 cups boiling water
1 cup cold water
¼ cup VODKA
¼ cup RUM
¼ cup BLACK RASPBERRY LIQUEUR
¼ cup TRIPLE SEC

Mix Gelatin with hot water until dissolved (approx 2 minutes). Add cold water, stir. Let sit until steam dissipates (no more than three minutes). Add Alcohol, Stir thoroughly (1-2 minutes). Pour mixture into your chosen Jello shot containers. Refrigerate for 4 hours or until firm. Makes 16-20 2oz Jello shots.

Vodka

Juicy Fruit

3 oz pkg Pineapple Jello
¾ cup boiling water
¼ cup cold water
1/3 cup VODKA
1/3 cup PEACH SCHNAPPS
1/3 cup MELON LIQUEUR

Mix Gelatin with hot water until dissolved (approx 2 minutes). Add cold water, stir. Let sit until steam dissipates (no more than three minutes). Add Alcohol, Stir thoroughly (1-2 minutes). Pour mixture into your chosen Jello shot containers. Refrigerate for 4 hours or until firm. Makes 8-10 2oz Jello shots.

Ecstasy

3 oz pkg Pineapple Jello
3 oz pkg Cranberry Jello
2 cups boiling water
1 cup cold water
½ cup VODKA
½ cup BLACK RASPBERRY LIQUEUR

Mix Gelatin with hot water until dissolved (approx 2 minutes). Add cold water and cola, stir. Let sit until steam dissipates (no more than three minutes). Add Alcohol, Stir thoroughly (1-2 minutes). Pour mixture into your chosen Jello shot containers. Refrigerate for 4 hours or until firm. Makes 16-20 2oz Jello shots.

Green Demon

3 oz pkg Lemon Jello
¾ cup boiling water
¼ cup cold water
1/3 cup VODKA
1/3 cup RUM
1/3 cup MELON LIQUEUR

Mix Gelatin with hot water until dissolved (approx 2 minutes). Add cold water, stir. Let sit until steam dissipates (no more than three minutes). Add Alcohol, Stir thoroughly (1-2 minutes). Pour mixture into your chosen Jello shot containers. Refrigerate for 4 hours or until firm. Makes 8-10 2oz Jello shots.

Vodka

Screwdriver

3 oz pkg Orange Jello
1 cup boiling water
½ cup cold water
½ cup VODKA

Mix Gelatin with hot water until dissolved (approx 2 minutes). Add cold water, stir. Let sit until steam dissipates (no more than three minutes). Add Alcohol, Stir thoroughly (1-2 minutes). Pour mixture into your chosen Jello shot containers. Refrigerate for 4 hours or until firm. Makes 8-10 2oz Jello shots.

Spryte

3 oz pkg Lemon Jello
3 oz pkg Lime Jello
2 cup heated Apple Juice (heat to just before boiling)
1 cup cold water
1 cup VODKA

Mix Gelatin with hot Apple Juice until dissolved (approx 2 minutes). Add cold water, stir. Let sit until steam dissipates (no more than three minutes). Add Alcohol, Stir thoroughly (1-2 minutes). Pour mixture into your chosen Jello shot containers. Refrigerate for 4 hours or until firm. Makes 16-20 2oz Jello shots.

Vitamin B

3 oz pkg Cranberry Jello
3 oz pkg Peach Jello
2 cups boiling water
1 can Red Bull
1 cup VODKA

Mix Gelatin with hot water until dissolved (approx 2 minutes). Red Bull, stir. Let sit until steam dissipates (no more than three minutes). Add Alcohol, Stir thoroughly (1-2 minutes). Pour mixture into your chosen Jello shot containers. Refrigerate for 4 hours or until firm. Makes 16-20 2oz Jello shots.

<u>Vodka</u>

Comfortable Fuzzy Screw Against the Wall

3 oz pkg Orange Jello
¾ cup boiling water
¼ cup cold water
1/3 cup SOUTHERN COMFORT
1/3 cup PEACH SCHNAPPS
1/3 cup VODKA

Mix Gelatin with hot water until dissolved (approx 2 minutes). Add cold water, stir. Let sit until steam dissipates (no more than three minutes). Add Alcohol, Stir thoroughly (1-2 minutes). Pour mixture into your chosen Jello shot containers. Refrigerate for 4 hours or until firm. Makes 8-10 2oz Jello shots.

Re-fresher

3 oz pkg Lime Jello
1 cup boiling water
½ cup cold water
½ cup Vodka

Mix Gelatin with hot water until dissolved (approx 2 minutes). Add cold water, stir. Let sit until steam dissipates (no more than three minutes). Add Alcohol, Stir thoroughly (1-2 minutes). Pour mixture into your chosen Jello shot containers. Refrigerate for 4 hours or until firm. Makes 8-10 2oz Jello shots.

A kiss from your Cousin

3 oz pkg Apricot Jello
1 cup boiling water
½ cup cold water
½ cup VODKA
a splash of Bitters (optional)

Mix Gelatin with hot water until dissolved (approx 2 minutes). Add cold water, stir. Let sit until steam dissipates (no more than three minutes). Add Alcohol, Stir thoroughly (1-2 minutes). Pour mixture into your chosen Jello shot containers. Refrigerate for 4 hours or until firm. Makes 8-10 2oz Jello shots.

Vodka

Little Boy Blu

3 oz pkg Berry Blue Jello
1 cup boiling water
½ cup cold water
½ cup VODKA

Mix Gelatin with hot water until dissolved (approx 2 minutes). Add cold water, stir. Let sit until steam dissipates (no more than three minutes). Add Alcohol, Stir thoroughly (1-2 minutes). Pour mixture into your chosen Jello shot containers. Refrigerate for 4 hours or until firm. Makes 8-10 2oz Jello shots.

Blind Date

3 oz pkg Mixed Fruit Jello
1 cup boiling water
½ cup cold water
½ cup VODKA

Mix Gelatin with hot water until dissolved (approx 2 minutes). Add cold water, stir. Let sit until steam dissipates (no more than three minutes). Add Alcohol, Stir thoroughly (1-2 minutes). Pour mixture into your chosen Jello shot containers. Refrigerate for 4 hours or until firm. Makes 8-10 2oz Jello shots.

Comfortable Screw

3 oz pkg Orange Jello
1 cup boiling water
½ cup cold water
¼ cup SOUTHERN COMFORT
¼ cup VODKA

Mix Gelatin with hot water until dissolved (approx 2 minutes). Add cold water, stir. Let sit until steam dissipates (no more than three minutes). Add Alcohol, Stir thoroughly (1-2 minutes). Pour mixture into your chosen Jello shot containers. Refrigerate for 4 hours or until firm. Makes 8-10 2oz Jello shots.

Vodka

BFF

3 oz pkg Strawberry-Kiwi Jello
1 cup boiling water
½ cup cold water
½ cup Vodka

Mix Gelatin with hot water until dissolved (approx 2 minutes). Add cold water, stir. Let sit until steam dissipates (no more than three minutes). Add Alcohol, Stir thoroughly (1-2 minutes). Pour mixture into your chosen Jello shot containers. Refrigerate for 4 hours or until firm. Makes 8-10 2oz Jello shots.

Red Apple

3 oz pkg Lemon Jello
1 cup hot Apple Juice (heat to just before boiling)
¼ cup cold water
¼ cup Grenadine
½ cup VODKA

Mix Gelatin with hot Apple Juice until dissolved (approx 2 minutes). Add cold water and Grenadine, stir. Let sit until steam dissipates (no more than three minutes). Add Alcohol, Stir thoroughly (1-2 minutes). Pour mixture into your chosen Jello shot containers. Refrigerate for 4 hours or until firm. Makes 8-10 2oz Jello shots.

SGR (Slow Gentle Ride)

3 oz pkg Mixed Fruit Jello
1 cup boiling water
½ cold water
¼ cup COCONUT RUM
¼ cup VODKA

Mix Gelatin with hot water until dissolved (approx 2 minutes). Add cold water, stir. Let sit until steam dissipates (no more than three minutes). Add Alcohol, Stir thoroughly (1-2 minutes). Pour mixture into your chosen Jello shot containers. Refrigerate for 4 hours or until firm. Makes 8-10 2oz Jello shots.

Vodka

Sour Apple

3 oz pkg Lime Jello
¾ cup boiling water
½ cup cold water
½ cup VODKA
¼ cup APPLE PUCKERS

Mix Gelatin with hot water until dissolved (approx 2 minutes). Add cold water, stir. Let sit until steam dissipates (no more than three minutes). Add Alcohol, Stir thoroughly (1-2 minutes). Pour mixture into your chosen Jello shot containers. Refrigerate for 4 hours or until firm. Makes 8-10 2oz Jello shots.

Blue Islander

3 oz pkg Berry Blue Jello
1 cup boiling water
½ cup cold water
¼ cup VODKA
¼ cup ISLAND PUCKER

Mix Gelatin with hot water until dissolved (approx 2 minutes). Add cold water, stir. Let sit until steam dissipates (no more than three minutes). Add Alcohol, Stir thoroughly (1-2 minutes). Pour mixture into your chosen Jello shot containers. Refrigerate for 4 hours or until firm. Makes 8-10 2oz Jello shots.

Chocolate Covered Cherry

3 oz Cherry Jello (or black cherry)
1 cup boiling water
½ cup cold water
¼ cup CHOCOLATE LIQUEUR
¼ cup VODKA

Mix Gelatin with hot water until dissolved (approx 2 minutes). Add cold water, stir. Let sit until steam dissipates (no more than three minutes). Add Alcohol, Stir thoroughly (1-2 minutes). Pour mixture into your chosen Jello shot containers. Refrigerate for 4 hours or until firm. Makes 8-10 2oz Jello shots.

Vodka

Melon Ball

3 oz pkg Pineapple Jello
1 cup boiling water
¼ cup cold water
½ cup VODKA
¼ Melon LIQUEUR

Mix Gelatin with hot water until dissolved (approx 2 minutes). Add cold water, stir. Let sit until steam dissipates (no more than three minutes). Add Alcohol, Stir thoroughly (1-2 minutes). Pour mixture into your chosen Jello shot containers. Refrigerate for 4 hours or until firm. Makes 8-10 2oz Jello shots.

Blue Lagoon

3 oz pkg Lemon Jello
1 cup boiling water
¼ cup cold water
½ cup VODKA
¼ cup BLUE CURACOA

Mix Gelatin with hot water until dissolved (approx 2 minutes). Add cold water, stir. Let sit until steam dissipates (no more than three minutes). Add Alcohol, Stir thoroughly (1-2 minutes). Pour mixture into your chosen Jello shot containers. Refrigerate for 4 hours or until firm. Makes 8-10 2oz Jello shots.

Polynesian Cocktail

3 oz pkg Lime Jello
1 cup boiling water
¼ cup cold water
½ cup VODKA
¼ cup BRANDY

Mix Gelatin with hot water until dissolved (approx 2 minutes). Add cold water, stir. Let sit until steam dissipates (no more than three minutes). Add Alcohol, Stir thoroughly (1-2 minutes). Pour mixture into your chosen Jello shot containers. Refrigerate for 4 hours or until firm. Makes 8-10 2oz Jello shots.

Vodka

Sex on The Beach

3 oz pkg Cranberry Jello
3 oz pkg Orange Jello
2 cups boiling water
½ cup cold water
¾ cup PEACH SCHNAPPS
¾ cup VODKA

Mix Gelatin with hot water until dissolved (approx 2 minutes). Add cold water, stir. Let sit until steam dissipates (no more than three minutes). Add Alcohol, Stir thoroughly (1-2 minutes). Pour mixture into your chosen Jello shot containers. Refrigerate for 4 hours or until firm. Makes 16-20 2oz Jello shots.

Sweet – n- Sour

3 oz pkg Lime Jello
¾ cup boiling water
½ cup cold water
¼ cup TRIPLE SEC
½ cup VODKA

Mix Gelatin with hot water until dissolved (approx 2 minutes). Add cold water, stir. Let sit until steam dissipates (no more than three minutes). Add Alcohol, Stir thoroughly (1-2 minutes). Pour mixture into your chosen Jello shot containers. Refrigerate for 4 hours or until firm. Makes 8-10 2oz Jello shots.

Pirates Bounty

3 oz pkg Grape Jello
3 oz pkg Pineapple Jello
3 oz pkg Lime Jello
2 cups boiling water
1 cup cold water
1 ½ cup COCONUT RUM
1 ½ cup VODKA

Mix Gelatin with hot water until dissolved (approx 2 minutes). Add cold water, stir. Let sit until steam dissipates (no more than three minutes). Add Alcohol, Stir thoroughly (1-2 minutes). Pour mixture into your chosen Jello shot containers. Refrigerate for 4 hours or until firm. Makes 24-30 2oz Jello shots.

Vodka

Harvey Wallbanger

3 oz pkg Orange Jello
1 cup boiling water
¼ cup cold water
½ cup VODKA
¼ cup GALLIANO

Mix Gelatin with hot water until dissolved (approx 2 minutes). Add cold water, stir. Let sit until steam dissipates (no more than three minutes). Add Alcohol, Stir thoroughly (1-2 minutes). Pour mixture into your chosen Jello shot containers. Refrigerate for 4 hours or until firm. Makes 8-10 2oz Jello shots.

Sex with a straw

3 oz pkg Strawberry Jello
1 cup boiling water
½ cup cold water
¼ cup STRAWBERRY SCHNAPPS
¼ cup VODKA

Mix Gelatin with hot water until dissolved (approx 2 minutes). Add cold water, stir. Let sit until steam dissipates (no more than three minutes). Add Alcohol, Stir thoroughly (1-2 minutes). Pour mixture into your chosen Jello shot containers. Refrigerate for 4 hours or until firm. Makes 8-10 2oz Jello shots.

Smooth –n- Easy

3 oz pkg Strawberry Jello
1 cup boiling water
¼ cup cold water
½ cup VODKA
¼ cup CRÈME DE BANANA

Mix Gelatin with hot water until dissolved (approx 2 minutes). Add cold water, stir. Let sit until steam dissipates (no more than three minutes). Add Alcohol, Stir thoroughly (1-2 minutes). Pour mixture into your chosen Jello shot containers. Refrigerate for 4 hours or until firm. Makes 8-10 2oz Jello shots.

Vodka

Robins Nest

3 oz pkg Cranberry Jello
1 cup boiling water
¼ cup cold water
½ cup VODKA
¼ cup CRÈME DE COCOA (white)

Mix Gelatin with hot water until dissolved (approx 2 minutes). Add cold water, stir. Let sit until steam dissipates (no more than three minutes). Add Alcohol, Stir thoroughly (1-2 minutes). Pour mixture into your chosen Jello shot containers. Refrigerate for 4 hours or until firm. Makes 8-10 2oz Jello shots.

Purple Mask

3 oz pkg Grape Jello
1 cup boiling water
¼ cup cold water
½ cup VODKA
¼ cup CRÈME DE COCOA (white)

Mix Gelatin with hot water until dissolved (approx 2 minutes). Add cold water, stir. Let sit until steam dissipates (no more than three minutes). Add Alcohol, Stir thoroughly (1-2 minutes). Pour mixture into your chosen Jello shot containers. Refrigerate for 4 hours or until firm. Makes 8-10 2oz Jello shots.

Top Banana

3 oz pkg Orange Jello
1 cup boiling water
¼ cup cold water
½ cup VODKA
¼ cup CRÈME DE BANANA

Mix Gelatin with hot water until dissolved (approx 2 minutes). Add cold water, stir. Let sit until steam dissipates (no more than three minutes). Add Alcohol, Stir thoroughly (1-2 minutes). Pour mixture into your chosen Jello shot containers. Refrigerate for 4 hours or until firm. Makes 8-10 2oz Jello shots.

Vodka

Fuzzy Navel

3 oz pkg Lime Jello
3 oz pkg Lemon Jello
2 cups boiling water
½ cup cold water
¾ cup PEACH SCHNAPPS
¾ cup VODKA

Mix Gelatin with hot water until dissolved (approx 2 minutes). Add cold water, stir. Let sit until steam dissipates (no more than three minutes). Add Alcohol, Stir thoroughly (1-2 minutes). Pour mixture into your chosen Jello shot containers. Refrigerate for 4 hours or until firm. Makes 16-20 2oz Jello shots.

Pineapple Upside Down Cake

3 oz pkg pineapple Jello
¾ cup boiling water
¼ cup cold water
½ cup VODKA
¼ cup IRISH CRÈME
¼ cup BUTTERSCOTCH SCHNAPPS

Mix Gelatin with hot water until dissolved (approx 2 minutes). Add cold water, stir. Let sit until steam dissipates (no more than three minutes). Add Alcohol, Stir thoroughly (1-2 minutes). Pour mixture into your chosen Jello shot containers. Refrigerate for 4 hours or until firm. Makes 8-10 2oz Jello shots.

Naked Pretzel

3 oz pkg Pineapple Jello
¾ cup boiling water
¼ cup cold water
½ cup VODKA
¼ cup MELON LIQUEUR
¼ cup CRÈME DE CASSIS

Mix Gelatin with hot water until dissolved (approx 2 minutes). Add cold water, stir. Let sit until steam dissipates (no more than three minutes). Add Alcohol, Stir thoroughly (1-2 minutes). Pour mixture into your chosen Jello shot containers. Refrigerate for 4 hours or until firm. Makes 8-10 2oz Jello shots.

Vodka

Gentle Ben

3 oz pkg Orange Jello
¾ cup boiling water
½ cup cold water
¼ cup GIN
¼ cup TEQUILA
¼ cup VODKA

Mix Gelatin with hot water until dissolved (approx 2 minutes). Add cold water, stir. Let sit until steam dissipates (no more than three minutes). Add Alcohol, Stir thoroughly (1-2 minutes). Pour mixture into your chosen Jello shot containers. Refrigerate for 4 hours or until firm. Makes 8-10 2oz Jello shots.

Long Island Iced Tea

6 oz pkg Lemon Jello (or two 3 oz packages)
1 cup boiling water
½ cup cola
½ cup cold water
½ cup GIN
½ cup LIGHT RUM
½ cup VODKA
½ cup TEQUILA

Mix Gelatin with hot water until dissolved (approx 2 minutes). Add cold water and cola, stir. Let sit until steam dissipates (no more than three minutes). Add Alcohol, Stir thoroughly (1-2 minutes). Pour mixture into your chosen Jello shot containers. Refrigerate for 4 hours or until firm. Makes 16-20 2oz Jello shots!

True Blue

3 oz pkg Berry Blue Jello
1 cup boiling water
½ cup cold water
½ cup BLUEBERRY VODKA

Mix Gelatin with hot water until dissolved (approx 2 minutes). Add cold water, stir. Let sit until steam dissipates (no more than three minutes). Add Alcohol, Stir thoroughly (1-2 minutes). Pour mixture into your chosen Jello shot containers. Refrigerate for 4 hours or until firm. Makes 8-10 2oz Jello shots.

Vodka

Very Cherry

3 oz pkg Cherry Jello
1 cup boiling water
½ cup cold water
½ cup CHERRY VODKA

Mix Gelatin with hot water until dissolved (approx 2 minutes). Add cold water, stir. Let sit until steam dissipates (no more than three minutes). Add Alcohol, Stir thoroughly (1-2 minutes). Pour mixture into your chosen Jello shot containers. Refrigerate for 4 hours or until firm. Makes 8-10 2oz Jello shots.

Alfie Cocktail

3 oz pkg Pineapple Jello
¾ cup boiling water
¼ cup cold water
¾ cup LEMON VODKA
¼ cup TRIPLE SEC

Mix Gelatin with hot water until dissolved (approx 2 minutes). Add cold water, stir. Let sit until steam dissipates (no more than three minutes). Add Alcohol, Stir thoroughly (1-2 minutes). Pour mixture into your chosen Jello shot containers. Refrigerate for 4 hours or until firm. Makes 8-10 2oz Jello shots.

Cordless Screwdriver

3 oz pkg Orange Jello
1 cup boiling water
½ cup cold water
½ cup ORANGE VODKA

Mix Gelatin with hot water until dissolved (approx 2 minutes). Add cold water, stir. Let sit until steam dissipates (no more than three minutes). Add Alcohol, Stir thoroughly (1-2 minutes). Pour mixture into your chosen Jello shot containers. Refrigerate for 4 hours or until firm. Makes 8-10 2oz Jello shots.

Vodka

Berry Fizz

3 oz pkg Strawberry Jello
¾ cup boiling water
½ cup cold water
½ cup RASPBERRY VODKA
¼ cup SPARKLING WINE

Mix Gelatin with hot water until dissolved (approx 2 minutes). Add cold water, stir. Let sit until steam dissipates (no more than three minutes). Add Alcohol, Stir thoroughly (1-2 minutes). Pour mixture into your chosen Jello shot containers. Refrigerate for 4 hours or until firm. Makes 8-10 2oz Jello shots.

Bottle Caps

3 oz pkg Lime Jello
1 cup boiling water
½ cup cold water
¼ cup RASPBERRY VODKA
¼ cup ROOTBEER SCHNAPPS

Mix Gelatin with hot water until dissolved (approx 2 minutes). Add cold water, stir. Let sit until steam dissipates (no more than three minutes). Add Alcohol, Stir thoroughly (1-2 minutes). Pour mixture into your chosen Jello shot containers. Refrigerate for 4 hours or until firm. Makes 8-10 2oz Jello shots.

The Freshman

3 oz pkg Lime Jello
1 cup boiling water
½ cup cold water
½ cup VANILLA VODKA

Mix Gelatin with hot water until dissolved (approx 2 minutes). Add cold water, stir. Let sit until steam dissipates (no more than three minutes). Add Alcohol, Stir thoroughly (1-2 minutes). Pour mixture into your chosen Jello shot containers. Refrigerate for 4 hours or until firm. Makes 8-10 2oz Jello shots.

Vodka

Orange Creamsicle

3 oz pkg Orange Jello
1 cup boiling water
½ cup cold water
½ cup VANILLA VODKA

Mix Gelatin with hot water until dissolved (approx 2 minutes). Add cold water, stir. Let sit until steam dissipates (no more than three minutes). Add Alcohol, Stir thoroughly (1-2 minutes). Pour mixture into your chosen Jello shot containers. Refrigerate for 4 hours or until firm. Makes 8-10 2oz Jello shots.

Berry Picker

3 oz pkg Strawberry Daiquiri Jello
1 cup boiling water
½ cup cold water
½ cup WATERMELON VODKA

Mix Gelatin with hot water until dissolved (approx 2 minutes). Add cold water, stir. Let sit until steam dissipates (no more than three minutes). Add Alcohol, Stir thoroughly (1-2 minutes). Pour mixture into your chosen Jello shot containers. Refrigerate for 4 hours or until firm. Makes 8-10 2oz Jello shots.

All Nighter

3 oz pkg Cherry Jello
1 cup boiling water
½ cup cold water
½ cup WATERMELON VODKA

Mix Gelatin with hot water until dissolved (approx 2 minutes). Add cold water, stir. Let sit until steam dissipates (no more than three minutes). Add Alcohol, Stir thoroughly (1-2 minutes). Pour mixture into your chosen Jello shot containers. Refrigerate for 4 hours or until firm. Makes 8-10 2oz Jello shots.

Sell this Book in your retail location

WWW.AVERAGEJOEPUBLISHING.COM

Also By Aaron Wright

PROMO'S 2 PROFITS

FUN, EASY, LOW COST BAR PROMOTIONS
PROVEN TO INCREASE SALES, BROADEN
CUSTOMER BASE, & MAXIMIZE PROFITS

BY

AARON WRIGHT